THE WATERFALL JOURNEY

A MANUAL OF BIBLICAL DISCIPLESHIP

Angie Coombes

ISBN: 978-0-9573098-2-1
For more information or to contact the author visit: **waterfalljourney.com**

TABLE OF CONTENTS

THE WATERFALL JOURNEY: A MANUAL OF BIBLICAL DISCIPLESHIP

HOW DO I DO THAT?

Throughout the book there are practical step by step sections to help us to travel side by side with the Holy Spirit and to understand His leading.

THE WATERFALL JOURNEY
A MANUAL OF BIBLICAL DISCIPLESHIP

PROLOGUE

Have you ever been really thirsty? The sort of thirst that comes with deserts and death, the kind of thirst that takes over your world so you can think of nothing else but cool, refreshing, crystal clear water. The sort of thirst that if it is not slaked but goes on with no remittance, changes your desire to any water, anything wet. Muddy, dirty, rank water would become as nectar. This is the kind of thirst that would drive you to the edge of madness, aching to be filled, tormented, desperately seeking the source of life.

What if, however, into this picture of arid, punishing emptiness there came someone who offered you a cup of clear, cool water? Then, as you finish that, a pail overflowing to quench your thirst, to slake the needs within you. Then more water for you to luxuriate in, a bathful to soak in and up. Then a place to stand under the thunder of a Niagara Falls so that there would be emptiness and thirst no more but water pouring in you, over you, and through you always.

Jesus met the Samaritan woman at a well outside the town as He was resting, awaiting the return of His disciples who had gone to find food. He asked her for a drink of water. Astonished that this stranger had even spoken to her, she questioned why He has asked and He replied:

> *You don't know what God wants to give you, and you don't know who is asking for a drink. If you did, you would ask me for the water that gives life.*
> *John 4:10*

Not understanding the significance of what He was saying she questioned His practical ability to draw water from the deep well with no bucket but Jesus was offering through the symbolism of water so much more:

Everyone who drinks this water will get thirsty again. But no one who drinks the water I give will ever be thirsty again. The water I give will become in that person a flowing fountain that gives eternal life. John 4:13-14

In Eden there was a Waterfall, a mighty outpouring, the River of the Water of Life flowing from the throne of heaven to the earth below. It was the flow of the Spirit that carried the sustenance of the Father to His beloved children, His very being to their very being. There were no spiritual thirsts.

Today thirsts are common to us all because in the Fall we were cut off from the drenching spring of living water, from replenishment in abundance. This is the spiritual death that God warned of when He forbade Adam and Eve to eat of the Tree of the Knowledge of Good and Evil in the Garden of Eden. Their disobedience and banishment from the Father's presence had far-reaching consequences for all mankind.

However, there was a rescue plan and the Father sent Jesus to draw us back to His presence. To the place where all our thirsts are slaked in the unimaginable magnitude of the Waterfall of living water, of love flowing from the Father to His children.

This book is about the unfolding understanding of my life experiences in the desert, of spiritual thirsts and of being starved of God which drove me for nearly half a century. It is about an incredible journey of travelling towards wholeness having been invited back into God's story, of opening up the high adventure that living back in relationship with the Father means in everyday life. My healing and the process of travelling back into the Waterfall became my ministry, sharing with others the heart of the Father for His children and the reality of who He wants us to be in His story.

....

BEGINNINGS

 I could not move. The evening sun was still warm on my face and the glow of a summer evening was thick about me. I stood leaning back against the sandstone of the building. I could feel the texture of the rock under my hands but I could not move. It was 9.15pm on a Thursday evening in Glasgow August 1991.

Five minutes earlier I had imploded. Half way through dinner quietly and devastatingly I had come to the end of me. I left my dinner companion, stumbled outside and leant against the wall. I was finished, I could not move. I felt like a jellyfish propped against the stone. Inside me there was nothing left just blackness, a numbing deep darkness. I was empty.

Paralysed and stuck I could do nothing. Time passed. In my head I whispered, "If you're there Jesus?" There was nothing else to do.

Then the God I had consciously banished from my life one day when I was washing up some twenty years previously – He came.

The God whom I had stamped on and dishonoured and obliterated from my life – He came.

HE CAME!

SPRINGS OF LIVING WATER

Rev. 22:17 THE SPIRIT AND THE BRIDE SAY 'COME!' AND LET HIM WHO HEARS SAY, 'COME!'. WHOEVER IS THIRSTY LET HIM COME; AND WHOEVER WISHES LET HIM TAKE THE FREE GIFT OF THE WATER OF LIFE.

Rev. 7:17 FOR THE LAMB AT THE CENTRE OF THE THRONE WILL BE THEIR SHEPHERD; HE WILL LEAD THEM TO SPRINGS OF LIVING WATER AND GOD WILL WIPE EVERY TEAR FROM THEIR EYES.

John 4:14 WHOEVER DRINKS THE WATER I GIVE HIM WILL NEVER THIRST. INDEED THE WATER OF LIFE WILL BECOME IN HIM A SPRING OF WATER WELLING UP TO ETERNAL LIFE.

Psalm 43:7 DEEP CALLS TO DEEP IN THE ROAR OF YOUR WATERFALLS.

Ezekiel 36:25 I WILL SPRINKLE CLEAN WATER ON YOU AND YOU WILL BE CLEAN. I WILL CLEANSE YOU FROM ALL YOUR IMPURITIES AND FROM ALL YOUR IDOLS. I WILL GIVE YOU A NEW HEART AND PUT A NEW SPIRIT IN YOU; I WILL REMOVE FROM YOU YOUR HEART OF STONE AND GIVE YOU A HEART OF FLESH. AND I WILL PUT MY SPIRIT IN YOU AND MOVE YOU TO FOLLOW MY DECREES AND BE CAREFUL TO KEEP MY LAWS. YOU WILL LIVE IN THE LAND I GAVE YOUR FOREFATHERS; YOU WILL BE MY PEOPLE AND I WILL BE YOUR GOD.

Ezekiel 47:9 SO WHERE THE RIVER FLOWS EVERYTHING WILL LIVE.

I was on a tour of Regional Claims centres doing a presentation on Positive Claims Handling, a racy little number that combined radical thinking with creative innovation all delivered with the energy and pizazz to get commercial liability claims handlers excited. No mean feat. It was a triumph that fed me appreciation and satisfaction. But …

I had arrived the day before and felt that with two nights at a hotel I had been given a holiday. As a high treat I thought I would buy myself a book so I took myself into WH Smiths to browse the shelves. I spent a long time choosing because I found it hard to justify the expense. Book in hand I joined the long queue at the till. As we shuffled forward my eye was caught by a display for the new Susan Howatch book 'Glittering Images' next to the till and at the last moment, without thinking, I swapped my book for hers. Outside on the pavement I was more than dumbfounded. My inner voice sneered, I couldn't even buy the book I wanted without messing up.

That Wednesday evening I began reading. 'Glittering Images' is about a clergyman, who was outwardly very successful but inwardly struggling. He acted a part to persuade the world otherwise so that no-one should know of the worthless wastelands within. The cost of keeping up the pretence became overwhelming. As he broke down there was a wise monk who worked with him on the road to recovery. As I read I was not only captured and fascinated by the central characters but also I became aware of a growing pain within me. I did not know what it was about but I did what I always did, I buried it. What I had read resonated with unfelt and unknown things that were deeply buried within me. I identified with the tension and exhaustion of years filled with a mismatch between my inner life and the outward performance.

The next day the successful presentation brought accolades and a sense of achievement, until 9.15pm.

HE CAME!

Dramatically, light came. The blackness dissolved and I was in and filled with a living glowing light. I had no doubt that Jesus had arrived. More than that I knew nothing but that I needed to find a church and my 'wise monk'. The reality of salvation for me was a living experience moving out of a tunnel of darkness and into the uplands of light.

'Glittering Images' was God's instrument in God's timing that brought me actively into God's story. God saving me that night was not my calling Him down into my story but Him lifting me up into a different part of His story, for I had a part to play for Him that no-one else could play. My time had come.

I came to understand that this was the turning point of my life, the beginning of my Waterfall Journey towards healing and wholeness. The contrast of before and after was so extreme and I was so grateful to God that I knew that I did not want to just sit in a pew. I thought I had wasted half my life and I was now sure that I wanted to make a difference for the rest of it.

ACKNOWLEDGEMENTS

There is a story to tell because of other people. None of us walks alone and I can only embark on this venture because I have travelled with many others who have imparted their wisdom and shared their learning, their tears and their company along the way.

My first church, led and taught by Roy and Una Barbour, was God's provision for me and the patience and encouragement of each person there, especially Raymond and Christine Noakes, were vital for a lost and broken beginner, with John and Janet Carter being especially significant. Here I met Phyllis Jewell who was my mentor, friend and prayer warrior and who taught me so much of the 'livingness' of God. I miss her.

My counsellor, Peter Addenbrooke, was my wise monk and he walked with me to the places of pain. Those years were my university, not only bringing understanding of my story but so much learning that has informed my ministry.

I owe much to CWR which was founded as a Christian ministry in 1965 by Selwyn Hughes. CWR is both an international publishing company and a training organisation, especially concerned with training Biblical Counsellors.

It was there God began building the platform for my ministry and brought me friendships that grew me and blessed me. Paul Grant gave me hope when I had none and an opportunity to be involved in tutoring at CWR and then, with Eileen his wife, a lasting friendship. Diana Priest helped me learn to be a friend and forgave my mistakes; my relationship with her is one of life's treasures. The team of tutors, especially those on the Introduction to Biblical Counselling course, grew from being colleagues to friends. Together with others God brought we allied ourselves as Pathway, determined travellers exploring life in the Waterfall. Clive Beach, Megan Billington, Mark and Alina Clark, Rosalyn Derges, Brian and Margaret Hagreen, John and Clare Henson, Mary Higginson, Brian and Carrol Keen, Prudence and Stephen Magee, and Jane Speake. All have blessed me and grown me.

Companions on ministry trips abroad helped fill my heart and expand my borders, Judith Bradley on three trips to Nepal and Irmgard Spittler for her vision out there; David and Rosemary Shaw over a dozen trips to Serbia staying with Ivan and Zorica Bozer; Heather MacDonald and Nicki-Sue Terry (née Leonard) for early trips to Uganda and Pam Laws for the last two trips out of the eight to Uganda when we reaped the harvest; out there Olivia Kyambadde , Jannet and Dan Opio, Pastor Sam Mukabi Zema, Pastor Tim and Dorcas Kibirige , Pastor Joshua , Pastor Franco and Faith, and so many more; and Margaret and Brian Hagreen for the opportunities in Kenya.

Richard Laws and I together have led the Introduction to Biblical Counselling course at CWR for many years and with his wife Pam now, as caring friends and learner painters we explore something of the third age together, paintbrushes at the ready.

I cannot name all from whom I have gained insights and encouragement without filling this book but I treasure each blessing for the enrichment of my life. It has not only come from people I have met but also books and preachers and courses and retreats. God's revelation and wisdom flows from so many channels and this small channel would not exist without them.

I need to acknowledge how I have grown working in my one to one ministry, each person sent by God has been used by Him for me too. I have been blessed and nourished even in giving. I am thankful for them all.

It is with joy that I thank Pam Hunt, a treasured friend in youth. We got lost in our middle years and now the friendship has been restored by God's design just when I was in need of a friend, a prayer warrior and help with this venture.

This book would still be locked in my computer and my heart without Paul Thompson. His unstinting gifts of time, expertise and encouragement have brought a raw manuscript to life. My grateful thanks to him and to his wife Gill for a constant supply of cake and coffee cannot be calculated.

Then there is my family, especially my children, Becci and Tim. They suffered in my wayward years, forgave and encouraged me in the healing years and now in a commune based on love we live in the proof of He will *restore the years the locusts have eaten* (Joel 2:25). This is for them and my grandchildren Noah, Wilfrid, Vincent, Isaac and Otto.

To all these and the many more I have not named my thanks for all you gave to me on this journey.

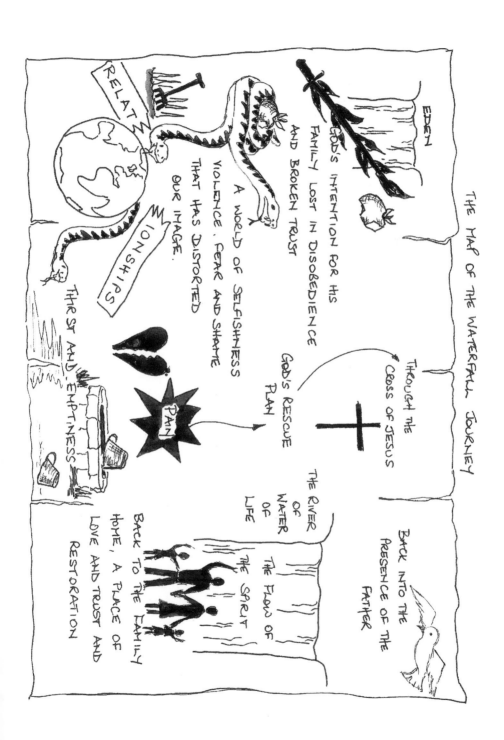

THE MAP OF THE WATERFALL JOURNEY

EDEN

GOD'S INTENTION FOR HIS
FAMILY LOST IN DISOBEDIENCE
AND BROKEN TRUST

A WORLD OF SELFISHNESS
VIOLENCE, FEAR AND SHAME
THAT HAS DISTORTED
OUR IMAGE.

RELAT IONSHIPS

THIRST AND EMPTINESS

GOD'S RESCUE
PLAN

PAIN

THROUGH THE
CROSS OF JESUS

BACK INTO THE
PRESENCE OF THE
FATHER

THE RIVER
OF
WATER
OF
LIFE

THE FLOW OF
THE SPIRIT

BACK TO THE FAMILY
HOME, A PLACE OF
LOVE AND TRUST AND
RESTORATION

PART ONE : FIRST THINGS

INTRODUCTION

The Waterfall Journey is about our life's adventure, being all our Lord and Creator designed us to be. In a deep and intimate relationship it takes us back to God's intention, the best that He has for us, living in close company with Him and involved in all His heart's purpose. The Waterfall Journey is a way to travel in His service and presence every moment of your life and so to achieve the significant purpose He has set before you.
We were created to travel with the Father on His business. We are going to explore what that looks like.

CHAPTER ONE

WHERE TO TRAVEL?

WHY AND HOW?

Not long ago I went on a retreat led by a pioneer of the revival of all things Celtic. It was a stimulating and insightful long weekend and the very mixed bunch from very mixed religious backgrounds were ardently seeking more of God. The last session was a discussion about 'thin places', those sacred places where through many years of prayer there seems to be an easier breaking through into God's presence. The last challenge to the group was to consider, "Are there 'thin people' who are readily able to access the presence of God?" The general consensus was that there were people who seemed to have a direct line to the Father but it seemed to be a mystery why this was so. We broke for the last meal and I went into the dining room surrounded by people asking, "How do you do that? How do you become a 'thin person'?"

 I felt the old surge of frustration often felt after conferences or sermons when I feel people have been sold short, left hanging because the doorway to the reality of what was shared has been left firmly closed.

The long refectory table was full and two of us sat on another table, apart. We talked. She was an Anglican from a pretty narrow field of experience but she was on fire to know more and how to move into what she was glimpsing. Alongside her enthusiasm was a despair of seeing something tantalising before her but not knowing how to grasp it. She had the feeling that when she went back to her church, no one would know what she had seen, let alone know how to become a 'thin person'.

I shared the Waterfall with her. In the time it took to eat a pudding, she was able to put all that she did know into a new perspective that gave her a way forward and the hope that she could be a 'thin person'. After all, it is why Jesus died on the Cross, to open up for each one of us the way that we might dwell in the presence of the Father, just as He did.

This has been the focus of my ministry over the years to help people experience the reality of a relationship with the living God, and to go on the Waterfall Journey serving His purposes and abiding in His presence.

Looking back on my life I can clearly see how in all the years up to my encounter with Jesus at forty-six the path I have followed has prepared me for this. God led me to pick up the skills, to see and to share the 'how of things' because I had so needed to know 'how' to come into that relationship with the heavenly Father myself.

My daughter runs an internet business of which I am the packing department. When learning all the computer work entailed in this I would get stressed until I understood how what I was doing fitted into the big scheme of things and how to do well the tasks to accomplish it. My daughter has many extraordinary gifts; teaching her mother is not one of them. She would give me too much information, too quickly but often not everything I needed and not in a usable order. I needed to know "How do I do that?" in a way that made sense to me, in a sequence that I could follow and reconstruct on my own.

If we are serious about journeying with God there are many things about which we need the "How do I do that?" processes. This is to be a practical book the 'how to' of a particular relationship, that of being a disciple of Jesus Christ. It is about bringing to life what we were created to enjoy, a living relationship with the three persons of Our God.

Why are many people in churches confined to their seats year after year not maturing in the faith, not actively walking as disciples? It seems for many it is because they do not know how to journey. They may hear what the relationship with God should be like but they do not know how to flow in a continually deepening experience of Him.

When Jesus stood on the mountain and gave His disciples the Great Commission:

All authority in heaven and on earth has been given to me. Therefore, go and make disciples of all nations, baptising them in the name of the Father and of the Son and of the Holy Spirit, and teaching them to obey everything I have commanded you. And surely I am with you always, to the very end of the age.
Matthew 28: 18-20

He spoke to men who had been grown and prepared in His presence, with His living example of relating to the Father and moving in the power of the Holy Spirit. When He said, *"Go and make disciples."* He was commanding that everything the first twelve had come to know about living and walking in the presence of the Father should be shared with all believers.

Often activity is the only way that people can translate their longing for God into a reality. Busy church programmes and endless good works do not deliver the spiritual connectedness that we desire. Many sit in church or go through life believing there should be more but not knowing what that looks like . As years pass they no longer expect or believe that a living relationship with God is possible or, even more damning, that it is for others and not for them.

Discipleship is about relationship. It's about God and His character and His purposes and it is about us aligning our story with His. The Waterfall Journey is understanding that story and being willing to step into it. It is all about God.

A vibrant, living relationship with the Father is the gift Jesus died to give us. Jesus had twelve disciples and thousands of followers; today if we obey His command in Matthew 28:18-19 the numbers should be very different. Disciples are 'thin people' aligned to the will and purposes of God and abiding in the presence of the Father as Jesus did. Today His church should be full of disciples.

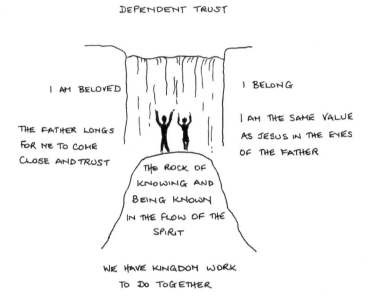

From the moment He saved me, God has taught me 'How to do that' in relation to my journey of discipleship. I have called this The Waterfall Journey and sharing these insights has become my ministry. They radically changed my life and when shared I see them doing the same for those who will embrace them.

Do you want to know you are living in the presence of the Father as Jesus did? Do you want to be used by God 24/7? Do you want to deepen your relationship with God? Do you want to live His way, from His perspectives and work alongside the living God? Well, that is what God wants too. This book is about being able to do that.

Jesus lived there, in the presence of the Father all the time and it was so important that He died to make it possible for us to do so too.

I have come to understand that it is WHERE I STAND to live my life that is key; it is that place of abiding that is so important. There I can know that I live every minute of my life God's way.

On the Waterfall Journey we will explore firstly HOW WE CAN FIND THE PLACE to be in The Father's presence and be aligned to His will and purpose, as Jesus demonstrated.

Secondly, we will explore the ways of overcoming the difficulties that would prevent us from experiencing all that we were born to be. What would rob us of our inheritance as God's children? There are three areas which throw us off track:

1. We may have a disjointed view of the Biblical story and do not see the big picture from God's perspective.
2. We may not know how to make what we do know come alive so that we can live it out in our daily lives.
3. Our pain may get in the way. Our distorted self-image and belief systems mean we misunderstand God's intentions.

This book is designed to help overcome these difficulties in practical ways.

Is being saved not enough? No, for it is only the start of the journey which takes us from being children of the world with all its ungodly distortions, to wholeness, to being all that we were individually designed to be.

Undoubtedly, God has unique paths for us all to tread and I am not suggesting we will all do things the same way but I pray that wherever you are now you will find within these pages ways to launch yourselves into new expressions of your relationship with The Father.

WAYS TO USE THIS BOOK

There are four elements to the content of this book.

1. We will look at some Biblical passages that give us a God perspective. There is a profound simplicity to everything we are going to share that often astounds people. *"Why did I not know that?"* is a question often asked by people hearing for the first time these truths after years of walking earnestly and faithfully. Usually everyone will already know a substantial amount and what we will share is the pivot that swings that understanding into a new landscape, just as a kaleidoscope reframes a new picture from what is already there.

2. We will keep looking at the *"How do I do that?"* God made His kingdom accessible. Sometimes religion makes it seem unreachable. So we will be looking at simple ways to open up new aspects of our understanding and most importantly, how to co-operate with the Holy Spirit as He seeks to teach us the ways of God which are presently hidden from us.

3. I will share some of my story. In my ministry, God has used my story in many ways and so there will be things I will share of it to illustrate my experience on the journey. The power of testimony is referred to in the New Testament as part of what will make us 'over-comers' of darkness. Your story and my story become part of God's armoury when we share the reality of the ups and downs we encounter as we follow Him.

4. I will suggest some areas for reflection, action or exploration that I found useful.

RECORDING YOUR JOURNEY

Recently, I went to Israel for the first time and as I customarily do I kept a journal. My goodness, the trip was not a holiday! We were doing fourteen hour days, beginning with a 6.30am breakfast and with precious few breaks we would 'do' site after site. I was exhausted but every evening I would write up the day, not only the places visited and the people seen but the impressions and the impact of being in the land God favoured and where Jesus walked. It has drawings and pictures and photographs.

From Bethlehem's Shepherds' Fields towards 1000 year old terraces, with olive trees, The Wall and an Israeli settlement beyond

Now when I pick it up as I do regularly it takes me back into the whole experience - I am there again. There were layers of things happening every moment and I am still discovering new aspects of those ten whirlwind days. If I had not kept the journal I would have lost much of what I was being given. It was hard enough to recall at the end of the day all the places we had been, the holiday from this time and distance would have been lost in blurred forgetfulness. However, all the richness is in the book, I have a treasure trove which will feed me for years.

God is beckoning us to join Him in the adventure that is His story and journalling can be very helpful for us to record our progress. The Waterfall Journey is a whole new way of relating to God and being involved with Him. It is about Him healing, equipping and growing us and journalling can help us understand better what is going on and to learn our part. It can be a resource for our future ministry. What you put in it and how you record it is up to you.

HOW DO I DO THAT?
RECORD MY JOURNEY

1. **CHOOSE A BOOK**: My family and I have a thing about stationery so choosing a book that I will take pleasure writing in would always be my starting point.
2. **ASK THE HOLY SPIRIT TO ASSIST YOU.**
3. **REVIEW EACH DAY:** God is going to open up many new ways to communicate with you. Look back on the day and find the messages He has left for you. It is akin to picking up pieces of a jigsaw and slotting them into their rightful place.
4. **RECORD THEM** in a way that is meaningful to you. You do not have to write reams. You might draw a picture or a mindmap, quote Scripture, be creative or simply list facts. Choose any way that allows you to have an overview on the page, to see the pattern of how God is leading you, to better understand your journey. Engage with questions and responses, pour out your heart's pain and wet the pages with your tears. Record your gratitude and praise. Make it your own.
5. **REVIEW:** Such a journal feeds and succours us as we grow in understanding but more than this, it opens up God's view and mind to us. This is about writing down what we have experienced and learning from it.

Two more points before we get started. The quotations used in the book are from the NIV Bible but there are so many rich translations available to be enjoyed which bring extra dimensions to understanding. I would encourage you to explore a range of Bibles once you have made one version your friend. I love The Message - the radical realism of its language breaks open new exciting ways to understand the Bible for me.

The second point is about the illustrations. My learning is enhanced by drawings as I have a strong visual component to the way I understand things. This is especially so if I have actually done the drawings myself. I have also seen God use these drawings to great effect in my ministry though I am no artist. All the illustrations used in this book mean something to me. I have an organic connection to them, they inform my journey in a deep way. Therefore, I have chosen not to reproduce them by mechanical means.

This book may be read straight through but also, as in a manual, you can look up areas of interest at will. However, I would suggest that you start with the first three chapters as God's Biblical perspective puts what follows into the context of His story.

THIS IS ALL ABOUT GOD FIRST

CHAPTER 2

GOD'S STORY

I love reading a good book. To be satisfying I need a book to have a beginning, a middle and an end, engaging characters, an exciting plot and I want to care about the outcome, to be involved in the way it ends.

The Bible is often described as a library of books that fall into different categories but the sum of the parts is so much more than this. It is 'Spirit breathed' and not one word is without relevance. It is more than a lifetime's work to understand its many layered wisdom.

The Bible is not a complete record of God's story though it does give us tantalising clues as to what went on before we made an entrance. It is the handbook detailing God's relationship with mankind and speaks of the over-arching purposes of God. Essentially, it is an amazing love story of God and His children and their Saviour.

Like all good books the Bible has plots and subplots, villains and heroes and you and I are invited to play a part too. It really helped me to understand the big picture of God's story so that I had an idea of the context of my own journey. It became clear whose story was the most significant. This was an eye opener because I had previously only thought about dragging God down into my life. Now I learned that my story was important in Kingdom terms when I joined God in his great enterprise. So let us explore this BIG PICTURE !

BEFORE THE BIBLE BEGAN

 We do not know a lot about God's story before the Bible began but we do know God and it is His character that is the engine that drives this story.

THE FATHER

THE SON   THE HOLY SPIRIT

ABIDING IN THE PRESENCE OF THE FATHER : ALIGNED TO THE WILL AND PURPOSE OF GOD

There was God whose essence was then, as it is now, LOVE. There was a heavenly kingdom characterised by the HARMONY flowing out from the Trinity and peopled by angelic beings. There was a hierarchy with angels and archangels and in the first subplot of God's story Lucifer, a favoured archangel, led a rebellion bringing discord to that realm. It was his pride and ambition which led him to want the power that he saw in the Most High:

> *How far you have fallen from heaven,*
> *O morning star, son of the dawn!*
> *You have been cast down to the earth*
> *You who once laid low the nations!*
> *You said in your heart,*
> *'I will ascend to heaven;*
> *I will raise up my throne above the stars of God;*
> *I will sit enthroned on the mount of assembly,*
> *On the utmost heights of the sacred mountains.*
> *I will ascend above the tops of the clouds;*
> *I will make myself like the Most High.'*
> *Isaiah 14: 12-14*

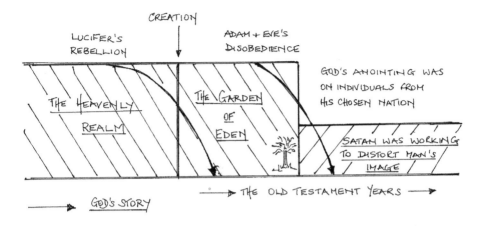

The contrast between Lucifer's five declarations of *"I will ..."* and the attitude of Jesus when tempted by the devil at the start of His ministry is stark. In Luke 4: 1-13 Jesus will not encroach into the area of His Father's authority.

The rebellion in heaven led to a battle and the defeat and banishment of the rebels.

> *And there was war in heaven. Michael and his angels fought against the dragon and the dragon and his angels fought back. But he was not strong enough and they lost their place in heaven. The great dragon was hurled down - that ancient serpent called the devil or Satan, who leads the whole world astray. He was hurled to the earth and his angels with him.*
> *Revelation 12:7-9*

So Satan and his minions were now upon earth, ejected from God's holy presence and determined to despoil all that God held dear.

THE SECOND SUB PLOT

In the meantime, because God is love and it is the nature of love that it has to be shared with others, a new plan was coming to fruition. As the Bible begins God has created a world of order and beauty for a family bearing His own image and He places them into a particular setting that will provide for them and bless them.

Genesis is where the two subplots collide. Satan and the rebel angels were roaming the earth having been evicted from heaven and God had placed His children, Adam and Eve, within the very specific boundaries of Eden. To them He now gave a commission to carry out on His behalf:

> *God blessed them and said to them, "Be fruitful and increase in number, fill the earth and subdue it."*
> *Genesis 1:28*

The children of light were destined when the race grew in numbers to move out beyond the borders of Eden and subdue the dark forces of Satan and the rest of the fallen angels that roamed the earth.

However, there are always setbacks in stories and the devil engineered one for Adam and Eve. Satan wanted to spoil God's plans and for the second time his strategy was to ferment rebellion and dissatisfaction in others by causing Adam and Eve to doubt God's goodness. God had given His children free will for He longed for them to choose to trust Him, not that they should be required like robots to obey a protocol.

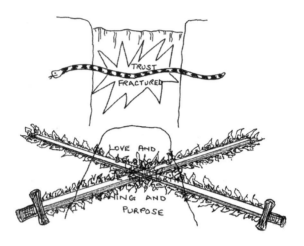

So they disobeyed God's one prohibition, not to eat of the Tree of the Knowledge of Good and Evil and sin came into the world fracturing relationships and trust. This rebellion too ended with an expulsion as Adam and Eve were put out of Eden, no longer able to remain in God's holy presence. God clothed them with skins and set a guard at the gate of Eden that they should not be tempted by the Tree of Life, as eternal life in their fallen state would have been purgatory for all time.

Now mankind, the devil and his minions all inhabited earth together. The devil's aim was to distort the image of God in His children as the effects of living in a world of broken relationships, with evil rampant, destroyed the harmony and love of God's intention.

THE RESCUE PLAN

Nevertheless, like all good stories where there is jeopardy, there is rescue. The Bible is the story of God's desire and plan to free His people.

The rescue plan unfolds through the Old Testament times. God did not give up on mankind. He chose a nation through which He would work. He chose ordinary people touched by the Holy Spirit to move His purposes forward, to prepare the way for Jesus, the Son of God who would pay the price to redeem the lost. It is the Cross and our cleansing by the blood of Jesus, through the forgiveness of our sins, that gives us the way back to enjoy the fullness of the relationship with the Father which was lost to us in the Fall.

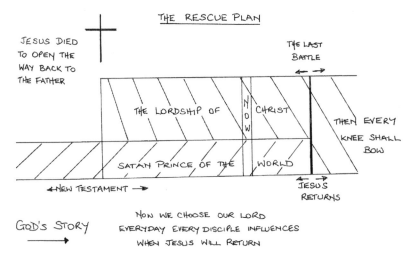

THE RESCUE PLAN

JESUS DIED TO OPEN THE WAY BACK TO THE FATHER

THE LAST BATTLE

THE LORDSHIP OF ⟨NOW⟩ CHRIST

THEN EVERY KNEE SHALL BOW

SATAN PRINCE OF THE WORLD

←NEW TESTAMENT →

JESUS RETURNS

GOD'S STORY →

NOW WE CHOOSE OUR LORD EVERYDAY EVERY DISCIPLE INFLUENCES WHEN JESUS WILL RETURN

Since Jesus won the victory over the devil on the Cross we have the choice about whom we choose to serve. We can choose to live under the Lordship of Christ or we live under the devil's bondage.

As Christians living in the fallen world we can be pulled in both directions. Jesus specifically prays for His disciples in John 17:14-19:

I have given them your word and the world has hated them, for they are not of the world any more than I am of the world. My prayer is not that you take them out of the world but that you protect them from the evil one. They are not of the world, even as I am not of it. Sanctify them by the truth; your word is truth. As you sent me into the world, I have sent them into the world. For them I sanctify myself, that they too may be truly sanctified.

Understanding this amazed me. There can be no doubt that evil is escalating in the world and that the devil is active in promoting his worldview where greed, envy, violence and hatred hold sway. However, I can choose where I stand to live my life and I choose to live under the authority of Jesus, where Kingdom values rule, where I am aligned to the will and purposes of God. This is life in the Waterfall and we are going to examine what that means in the next chapter.

For most Christians, they will sing and believe that Jesus is Lord on a Sunday morning but by the afternoon the pressures of life in the world have taken over. They sing of the majesty of God in their worship but in the afternoon they doubt whether He can aid them in their plans to survive. They know the character of God is about love and trust but they are not sure it includes them or how to experience Him in their own lives.

As we move towards the end times, what you and I do makes a difference in Kingdom terms as to when Jesus returns BECAUSE God has chosen to use mankind as the army to fight the last battle and to be the bride of Christ. Much has to happen to change the church into both a battle-ready force and a spotless bride before then. At present much of the army of God is in sickbay, too wounded, tired or burnt out to bear arms and not knowing how to operate under the command of its General.

How will we be ready? By each of us embarking on our own Waterfall Journey into true discipleship and as mature followers, living in the freedom of all Jesus died to restore to us and by following where He leads.

The climax of God's story is the final overthrow and rout of the devil after which *"every knee shall bow"* to the Lordship of Jesus. This heralds in the *"new heaven and new earth"* where we will enjoy life in its fullness as God's children, in chapters yet to be revealed

Having this overview of God's story helps us see that what happens day-by-day in our lives has relevance. Each day we can be advancing God's purposes if we are journeying under Christ's direction. This is a co-operative venture between God and His children because He chooses for it to be so. The Waterfall Journey is significant for God's story because it is about how we respond to His invitation to be part of His higher purposes.

REFLECTION
Our response to God's invitation to join His story matters because:

1. As individuals, our journey to restoration and growth into our full potential and gifting matters to the fulfilment of God's purposes.
2. For us to play our full part in the story, we must know God's perspectives and be aligned with them.
3. Fulfilling our purpose has a direct bearing on when the return of Jesus will take place and
4. As we journey, our relationship to the Father will blossom into all it was intended to be.

So consider your response in each area.

Review where you are on your journey.

We will all be starting from different points along the way and it is very useful to explore the landscape at this your starting place.

Where are you right now in your life?

What is good?

What is difficult?

Where are the blessings?

What is missing?

What is going on inside you?

Where is God in the picture?

You may find it helpful to record your reflections.

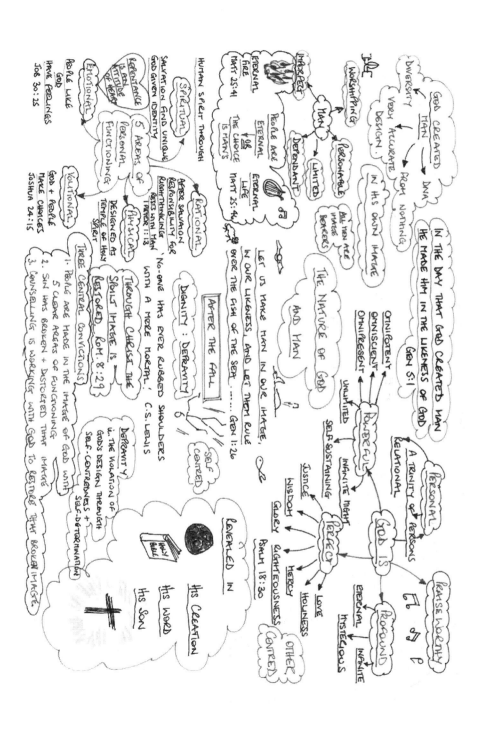

CHAPTER 3

THE WATERFALL

This book is about the journey of disciples who are deeply in love with God and who move and have their being in Him, in the Waterfall. The image of the Waterfall was a God-given picture of life abiding in the presence of Father, where we were designed to live. The foundation for this relationship comes from understanding what was going on in the first three chapters of Genesis. Here we see what God intended for His relationship with His children and what went wrong.

Simon sat on the sofa, his head in his hands. He was looking down, and moving his head from side to side and muttering wonderingly, "But I knew all this – so why didn't I know all this?" I was in Norway. It was a Friday evening and I had just shared God's story and the Waterfall with the group gathered for the first session of a weekend. Simon was blown away as the others were by the new perspectives and possibilities of what they had just seen and heard. It was not that they did not know the first three chapters of Genesis. It was that suddenly they were now seeing God's view and how the Fall had so radically affected their lives.

GOD'S INTENTION FOR HIS CHILDREN

God is love and it is the nature of love that it has to be shared. God so wanted a family to love that He made us in His image, sharing His family likeness. God is excited about us. We see a reflection of this when a new baby is born into our family. I am writing this the week an heir to the throne has been born. What a wild jamboree! The media have been in a frenzy but William and Kate have turned aside and gone away for a time of quiet, to bond with their son. God wanted that too, a special place where intimacy would be established. Eden. What we feel and long for has come to us from Him. This is not a detached Father who parents us from a distance; all that desire for involvement, closeness and emotional attachment are His too.

In preparation for His children God readied the earth and within very precise boundaries, there within the Garden of Eden He placed them. God did not hold back in creating the perfect setting: full of colour and texture, sights and sounds and smells to delight, with flowers and trees, animals and birds. What an overload to the senses! Today none of us can be unaware of the wonders and intricacies of the natural world brought to our television screens or actually experienced on some exotic holiday. Truly awesome and magical images from any David Attenborough series give us some sense of the extravagance of the provision from our God, who wanted the best for His children.

Then the act of bringing us His children into being, was not a detached process. On the sixth day the Garden ready, God created His family:

So God created man in his own image, in the image of God created him; male and female he created them.
Genesis 1:27

This means we share God's nature, character and DNA. We are emotional, rational and spiritual just as He is; we can make choices, we are family.
How He created us is powerfully described in Genesis:

The Lord God formed the man from the dust of the ground and breathed into his nostrils the breath of life, and the man became a living being.
Genesis 2: 7

This is a picture of a very intimate connection between a loving Father and His children. He bends, He gathers, He breathes and with His life gives us life.

....

DON'T MAJOR ON IT!

I used to worry a lot about where the truth of creation was to be found but I have come to realise that there are many things that are a mystery to me. Now I am very comfortable with that but I used to be embarrassed. I would avoid any discussion because I did believe we are uniquely created in the image of God and not that we evolved from apes. I also believe in what science has discovered, even if I do not always believe in the scientists' interpretation. So I was left stranded hoping no-one would challenge me to reveal what I thought. I found Derek Prince helpful. He said that in the passage of evolution at the right time and in the right place God placed His children, the Adamic race into the world. That made sense to me and fitted all the evidence. I have peace with that.

Much of what I learned in the early years of my walk was filtered through the wisdom of my friend Phyllis. She was an inspiration and helped me see kingdom perspectives. When you are growing you need others around you to offer you their wisdom. Things Phyll said to me are burned into my brain and I repeat them for those whom I meet along the way. Though no longer here, I can still hear her saying, "DON'T MAJOR ON IT!" It was such a help because it means that if I do not understand or if I'm stuck with a behaviour I'm not changing or I am struggling in a hole, I don't major on it. I trust God in His time will reveal the missing understanding or will help me change or will rescue me. My job is to keep trusting, to keep following and to learn from the process, as well as the content of the journey.

What do I mean by that? It is this. God is always working with us on many levels. If I am having a struggle, the experience of struggling is as much part of my learning as the eventual victory.

The Waterfall Journey is equipping and training you as you travel.

> Praise be to the God and Father of our Lord Jesus Christ, the Father of compassion and the God of all comfort, who comforts us in all our troubles, so that we can comfort those in any trouble with the comfort we ourselves receive from God. For just as we share abundantly in the sufferings of Christ, so also our comfort abounds through Christ.
> 2 Corinthians 1: 3-5

Collecting knowledge and placing it in my understanding so that it becomes part of me has built up the spiritual landscape through which I have travelled. Some things I have seen clearly, maybe relatively quickly; other truths just drop into my mind unbidden. Other truths have only emerged from the mists after much searching. We are not spoon-fed everything we need. God wants us to learn, to seek, to explore, to build up spiritual muscle to travel.

There are three truths to grasp and relax into. Firstly, in the Waterfall the Holy Spirit will lead you to the truth God is setting before you; secondly, if you are willing and co-operating God has the perfect timing for you to understand. Then, most importantly there is a promise to hold on to:

> The Lord will fulfil His purpose for me.
> Psalms 138:8

He will get you there! Meanwhile don't major on it!

In Genesis the love the Father had for Adam and Eve is seen not only in the environment He provided but in the relationships that are portrayed there. God set the safe boundaries but within those He gave responsibility to Adam. When He asked Adam to name the animals it was a co-operative venture and it must have been fun. As each animal appeared Adam took authority and gave it a name. Elephant... armadillo ... kangaroo ... he was joining God in creation because when you name a thing, you set something of its character.

When this work was done and there was no helper for Adam God caused sleep to fall upon him and He met Adam's deepest need by fashioning woman from his ribs. God was working on so many levels. There was a connectedness between Adam and Eve because as he said,

> *This is now bone of my bones flesh of my flesh; and she shall be called woman*
> *for she was taken out of man.*
> *Genesis 2:23*

This union was to be the foundation for ongoing family life. With two individuals God was initiating marriage BUT He was still central in the picture. The trinity in marriage was to mirror the love and selflessness of the Godhead.

God was present providing His blessing, His kingdom values ruled in the Garden, nakedness was freedom and innocence flowed from the hearts of Adam and Eve in simple profound trust. There was a joy in each other, to be shared as in the cool of the evening the Father came to walk and talk with them.

THE WATERFALL

This was the place where we were born to live, abiding in the presence of the Father and the image of the Waterfall gives a dramatic picture of the reality of the flow of love from Him to us. The love of the Father is awesome, flowing into and through His children. In the overflow of that vertical outpouring, horizontal relationships flourish into everything they were meant to be:

> *Deep calls to deep in the roar of your waterfalls. Psalm 42:7*

It is also symbolic of the deep spiritual connection through which every need of life is sustained in us, the children of the Father.

The living water gave Adam and Eve a secure foundation, an experience of having all their needs fully satisfied within that relationship with the Father.

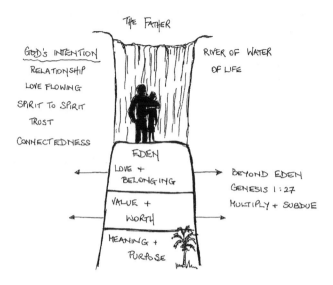

We are all created to be sustained by the Father in three crucial areas:-

1. **To know we are unconditionally LOVED and so we have a place where we BELONG**
2. **To know we are VALUED as a person and have WORTH in the eyes of others**
3. **To know that our life has MEANING and PURPOSE, that our being will make a difference.**

....

I was in Uganda with Heather. In front of us were 90 new recruits to the Police Force. They had been marched in with shaved heads and baggy khaki boiler suits. A sergeant lurked in the background. God was not to be mentioned but we were to spend time thinking about 'Vision and Values'. We did some fun things and during the day wariness became enjoyment and eventually passion.

One of the questions we asked was "What matters to you?" Discussions and lists were refined until they had the three things that mattered most to each of them. What startled them was discovering they all had the same three. What shocked them was the realisation that these were universal and that all those they would be dealing with would also care deeply about these things. One girl summed it up, "This is going to change the way I will do my job. I had not thought that the people we are going to be dealing with are like me, wanting what I want."

So what did they come up with? It was no surprise. Firstly, they wanted a home and family, where they loved and were loved, a place of belonging and connectedness. Secondly, they wanted to be recognised as being of value by others and they would know this by the way they were treated. In turn they wanted to have self-respect, a sense of identity and to know their own worth. Thirdly, they wanted to do a meaningful job well, to have pride in what they did and to know that it would be significant, it would make a difference. We could not mention God but they did and there was a general consensus that this meant 'walking as Jesus walked.'

This was in 2003. The Ugandan police force had been a laughing stock, ineffective and corrupt, many serving with little hope and troublesome behaviours. There was a new leadership with radical ideas and some wonderful local Christians, led by Olivia, Pastor Sam, Pastor Tim and Pastor Joshua, who were called by God to invest their energy and talents into the men and women who would serve in the force.

In the course of our one day we saw people who had been bashful about being in the police being inspired to be involved in something special as they sought to fulfil the God-given needs within themselves. They were recognising that we are designed for higher purposes.

In the years since, every recruit in their first year of basic training has a week run by this team of local Christians, whose own lives and ministries were radically altered by the Waterfall Journey. Many of the recruits come from very difficult backgrounds, Uganda's family structures having been devastated by Aids. They explore their histories and receive counselling, experiencing healing and transformation. Why? Because in practice they know they are being LOVED and they are part of the force family. They BELONG. Their VALUE is evident by the care being given to their stories and the way they are treated and their feeling of WORTH rockets with individual attention to their needs. They explore MEANING and PURPOSE, the higher significance of their lives and the vision of making a difference for their nation. The Police force has changed; the Commander puts it down in large part to the results this week has on his people.

NOTES

ACTIVITY
Try an exercise for yourself.

With our recruits in Uganda we encouraged them to identify what they valued above all else in their life.
Just sit quietly and try and get in touch with what you feel about yourself and life.
Brainstorm a list of all the things that you value from life.
- What are the deal breakers – those things you cherish, that would make life intolerable, if they were not present for you?
- Are you using your time and energy on the things that most matter to you?
- Where is God in this?
- Do you know His view on this?
- Do there need to be changes?

Refine the list down to 10 things and then further reduce it to 3.
How are you doing in these 3 areas?
Do your values align with the values of the Kingdom?

You may find it helpful to record your reflections.

Let's go back to the story in Eden; here in the Waterfall of God's love, Adam and Eve were filled by Him to overflowing, allowing them to have full and satisfying relationships with each other. The vertical relationship with the Father was the key to deep and perfect harmony between human beings. Relationships were maintained by sharing thoughts and feelings. When sharing time in the cool of the evening, walking together, there were things to talk about for God had not created Adam and Eve for idleness:

> *The Lord God took the man and put him in the Garden of Eden to work it and take care of it. Genesis 2:15*

However, this was only part of the work planned; the first commission given to mankind points to the higher purposes of God:

> *God blessed them and said to them, "Be fruitful and increase in number, fill the earth and subdue it. Rule over the fish of the sea and the birds of the air and over every living creature that moves on the ground."*
> *Genesis 1:28*

The children of God, as children of the light, were supposed to move out from the Garden to fill and subdue the earth, recovering it from the devil and his minions, who had been thrown out of the heavenly realms and down to earth. Light was to overcome the darkness. Thus, the Garden is a picture of trust, intimacy and richness, sublime relationships in a sublime landscape where God's children were aligned to His will and purposes. There was just one boundary that God set:

You are free to eat from any tree in the garden, but you must not eat from the tree of the knowledge of good and evil, for when you eat of it you will surely die. Genesis 2:16

THE TWO SUBPLOTS OF GOD'S STORY COLLIDE

Satan is immediately alert to an opportunity. In Genesis, Satan in the form of a serpent determines to spoil not only the relationship between the Father and His children but also the family likeness. To distort the image bearers, in a savage thrust into the heart of God, he attacks:

Did God really say, "You must not eat from any tree in the garden?" Genesis 3:1

The command had been given directly to Adam but Satan gets Eve to focus on a tree which had always been a part of the landscape. He deliberately overstates God's command and she responds with a very accurate paraphrase of God's original statement. Satan then seizes his chance:

"You will not surely die" the serpent said to the woman. "For God knows that when you eat of it your eyes will be opened, and you will be like God, knowing good from evil." Genesis 3:4

Until this moment the richness of their surroundings had made Adam and Eve unaware of any deprivation but now Eve thinks about Satan's words and a seed of doubt is planted in her mind. Her attention is focused on the tree she looks at the fruit and wonders, *"Why not?"* She has no understanding of temptation or the spiritual death it will entail. Now, doubting God's absolute goodness and beginning to doubt the truth of God's words she decides that the fruit looks good; she cannot see why it would be harmful and indeed thinks it will bring wisdom.

When the woman saw that the fruit of the tree was good for food and pleasing to the eye, and also desirable for gaining wisdom, she took some and ate it. She also gave some to her husband, who was with her and he ate it. Genesis 3:6

A decision is made she eats and offers the fruit to Adam who is by her side throughout, a silent, compliant co-conspirator.

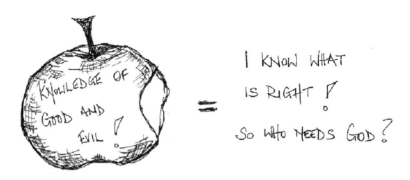

The devil always attacks us through our minds and desires. Adam and Eve in eating from the Tree of the Knowledge of Good and Evil have moved into the place which brings hurt and pain.

> **THEY THINK THEY KNOW BEST**
> **THEY THINK THEY KNOW GOOD FROM BAD**
> **THEY THINK THEY KNOW RIGHT FROM WRONG**

Now they can play God in their own lives and the lives of others. God is redundant; they are acting independently, making their own decisions. At a stroke everything is changed; trust is broken and sin floods into the world. The relationship with the Father is fractured. Sinful man is cut off from a holy God, the Father is no longer accessible. Adam and Eve have made a choice that will lead to great suffering.

THE CONSEQUENCES

Having broken God's trust, for their own safety God evicts Adam and Eve from Eden so that they do not eat of the Tree of Life.

Outside the Waterfall, exiled, they are alone and cut off from the flow of the Spirit. This is the death that God spoke about. Where there was fullness of love and stability, now there is emptiness and uncertainty.

> **What had been the absolute knowledge and experience of LOVE and BELONGING becomes loss and leads to feelings of being ALONE and ISOLATED.**
> **SECURITY was gone.**
>
> **What had been the absolute knowledge and experience of being VALUED and RESPECTED was lost, replaced by feelings of being of NO VALUE and WORTHLESSNESS.**
> **SELF-WORTH was shattered.**
>
> **What had been the absolute knowledge and experience of knowing MEANING and PURPOSE was gone. The opposite was now true,**

everything seemed to be MEANINGLESS and to NO PURPOSE. SIGNIFICANCE was ended.

PAIN had entered the world and since the Fall there has been neediness and emptiness in man.

Living in the fallen world, running on empty instead of full tanks of love, we experience life like balancing on a pin instead of on the firm rock we were born to stand on.

This is the death that God warned against. We were born to live in the Waterfall of God's love - outside that we gasp like a stranded fish on a river bank. To survive in desperation we are driven to where we think we can satisfy our raging thirst for the lack of God. Jeremiah reveals the agony this is to God whose children have turned from Him to worthless idols.

Has a nation ever changed its gods? (Yet they are not gods at all.) But my people have exchanged their Glory for worthless idols. Be appalled at this O heavens, and shudder with great horror. Jeremiah 2:11

God makes it very clear what His children have done:

My people have committed two sins: they have turned away from me the spring of living water and dug their own cisterns, cisterns that cannot hold water. Jeremiah 2:13

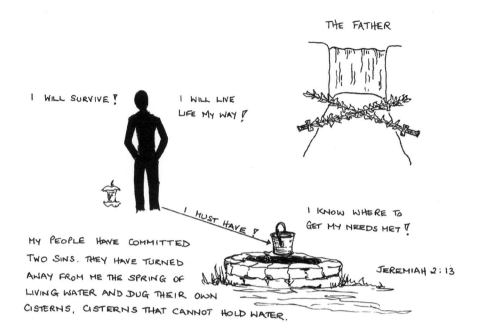

Having rejected life in the abundance of the Waterfall of God's love, in the fallen world all our behaviour drives us towards the bucket we put down into our cistern or well.

We have seen from the Ugandan recruits that all of us long for:

LOVE and BELONGING

VALUE and WORTH

MEANING and PURPOSE.

These are not casual requirements for our wellbeing but life itself, they are crucial for us and the thirst for them will drive us to our cisterns.

However, what goes in the bucket is not living water and the cistern leaks; there are droughts and we have to survive on what we can get. Always the raging thirst remains and we have pain and emptiness, not abundance.

NOTES

_____

_____

_____

_____

_____

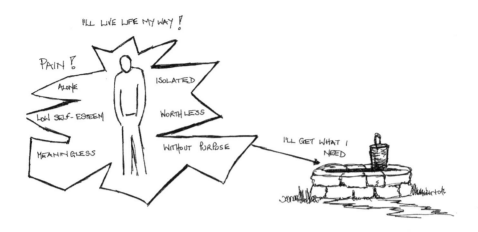

GOD'S RESCUE PLAN

When God created his children He signalled the importance of the relationship He wanted to enjoy with us by giving us free will. He wanted us to choose His way through trust and love. The wrong choice was made in the Garden by Adam and Eve which meant that the way of redemption was going to be long and arduous.

Sin was in the world, therefore the choice of the path to the Waterfall was cut off by sinfulness which could not be taken into the Father's holy presence.

SIN WAS THE PROBLEM.

However, even though God had exiled His children He was working His purposes out to make a way back. God was with His people every step of the way.

Under the Law in the Old Testament God made provision for the forgiveness of sin by a complex series of sacrifices to cover all eventualities. Blood had to be spilt by animal sacrifices that needed to be ongoing, some in the set pattern that God gave to Moses, others for individual occurrences. In addition, access to the presence of God in the Most Holy Place was only allowed to the priest after ritual cleansing and only once a year. The penalty for breaking these laws was death. The Israelites were taught by God to be in awe of His holiness and to deal with sin.

Wonderfully, throughout the Old Testament God was preparing the ground and pointing the way for His rescue plan to come into being which would allow His people to live again in all the fullness of the relationship that He intended to have with them.

The Father provided the sacrifice in Jesus, who once and for all time paid the price for our sin. It cost the Father to send His beloved Son and it cost Jesus to become the blood sacrifice for us. We can only glimpse the pain involved within the Trinity but for our God the price was worth it. Amazingly, we were worth it to Him. Do you hear that? It will change your life when you drink that in instead of letting it float over your head. It is all about God, not us.

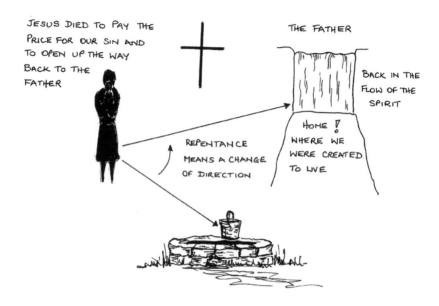

He said we were worth it to Him, full stop. Nowhere did He say we have to be worthy! Jesus came to rescue sinners, He knew the condition we were in. Jesus died for us taking the penalty for our sin that we might be cleansed and forgiven, free to choose to live abiding in the presence of the Father.

We have now two clear choices; there are two places to stand to access those things we need to sustain us. We can stand in the full flow of the River of the Water of Life cascading in the Waterfall, as Jesus did when He walked on earth or we can take the path to the well, to the thirst which comes from leaking dregs from a broken cistern. All of us were born into the fallen world and we will see later how we became wounded, and in our pain and emptiness we have constructed our own irrigation systems to survive outside the Father's presence. However, now, because of Jesus and His sacrifice, we can take the new path back into the Waterfall.

The church is hesitant to name things as sin in today's liberal culture. However, once we recognise that something in our behaviour is sinful we can know what to do. We can turn away from the cistern, acknowledging

our independence

our reliance on idols

our sinful choices

and turning through repentance, into the forgiveness that Jesus bought for us on the Cross we can stand again in the presence of the Father. We can come home.

RECOGNITION OF SIN leads to
  REPENTANCE and turning to
    THE FATHER FOR FORGIVENESS
      THROUGH THE CROSS OF JESUS
        INTO THE WATERFALL OF THE
          FATHER'S PRESENCE

IT IS WHERE YOU CHOOSE TO LIVE YOUR LIFE THAT COUNTS.

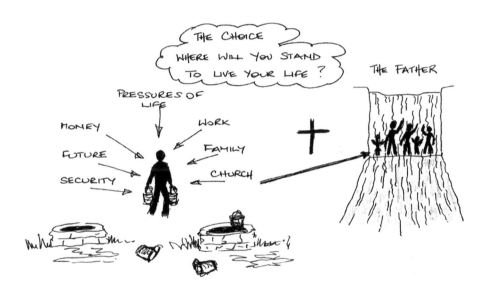

Jesus as He went back to the Father, said *"Make disciples."* The place of discipleship is in the Waterfall of God's love; it is where Jesus walked when on earth. It is being directly connected to Heaven in the flow of the Spirit. Jesus did what His Father gave Him to do and said the words the Father gave Him to say, that is doing and saying what came into His head and His heart.

It is the place where we are on the team, working in co-operation with the living God, walking as Jesus walked. It is not a sinecure. The life of a disciple is not an easy one. However, it is the greatest adventure. It is where we were born to live and where we will be everything we were created to be.

SO WHERE DO YOU STAND TO LIVE YOUR LIFE?

IN THE FALLEN WORLD	or	IN THE WATERFALL OF GOD'S LOVE
Surviving somehow		Trusting God
Believing in yourself		Believing in God's goodness
Trying to control life		Living in the restored flow of the Spirit
Driven by woundedness		Fast-tracked to healing and wholeness
Striving to be someone		In a restored relationship with the Father
Thirsting and emptiness within		Discipled by Jesus
Thinking you know best		Abiding in rest and peace
Exhaustedly 'doing'		Fulfilling your God-given destiny

LIFE IN THE WATERFALL

The Waterfall is the place where we again choose to trust that God is good all the time. For many it seems to be such a risk to step into this place when they have been kicked by the world and relied on themselves for survival. Is God to be trusted?

I had been having counselling for about six years. Twice a week I saw my counsellor and I had understood much about my story but I was stuck. Then I went on a three week introduction to counselling course at Waverley Abbey House run by CWR, the organisation set up by Selwyn Hughes. Selwyn was a pastor with a heart for God and his people and who had with Larry Crabb produced a model to help hurting people see God's way. When I saw that model drawn out, the light came on for me. I saw at once I was trying to play God in my life and knew the awful consequences that it had caused for me and others.
I understood immediately that I had a choice about where I stood to live my life. It was a revelation that changed everything and would be transformed into my ministry as I lived out what was to become 'The Waterfall Journey.' Since 2001 at home and abroad I have watched God switch on the light for countless others.

There was an old black and white film starring David Niven that told the story of breaking the sound barrier. In those days planes were controlled by a joystick. The pilot pulled back on the stick to bring the nose of the aircraft up to climb and pushed it forward to dive. Several aircraft were lost at the point of breaking the sound barrier because the planes went into an unstoppable dive even when the pilots were pulling back on the controls. David went up, tension crackled as he approached Mach One and as he hit the stall point the aircraft began to fall away but our plucky hero, defying all knowledge and experience, reversed the controls. He pushed the joystick forward, immediately the nose came up. All was well!

This is such a good picture of what making the commitment to trust God in the Waterfall is like. At the point of decision it feels to be a great risk because we have no evidence it is going to work. It defies all our knowledge about life. It denies all our experience and runs counter to our survival mode where we try to control everything to keep ourselves safe.

In the Waterfall I am saying, "I trust you God. I am aligning myself to your will and your purposes; you be God in my life." This is the place of discipleship. "I am taking my hands off the controls and I am going to follow you."

Home with the Father is only ever one step away. If we will commit to turning from the idols we have put in place of God and repent, if we are forgiven by the blood of Jesus and choose to trust God in the Waterfall WE ARE THERE. When John's disciples come and ask Jesus where He is staying He says, *"Come and see the place."*

Jesus is standing in the Waterfall saying, *"Come and see the place."*

My experience has been that if people will commit to life in the Waterfall God will unfold what it means to be there. So many things change. In subsequent chapters we are going to be exploring how to co-operate with the Holy Spirit as He heals and grows us there.
However, there are some immediate changes.

The place of abiding is where Jesus lived with the Father as He walked the earth. In the Waterfall is rest:

> In repentance and rest is your salvation, in quietness and trust is your strength. Isaiah 30:15

Trusting God for every area of life, family, health, security, job, finances and allowing God to be God in our lives, we enter the peace that the world cannot give. It is not a place of striving but of obedience. It is where disciples live. It changes life and turns upside down what has gone before in our lives. Life is now to be lived from God's perspective not our own. It is reversing the controls.

Now God can really do business with us.

Most of us Christians live out our lives in the fallen world, not trusting God for much though we sing differently for two hours on a Sunday! Then we go home and the burdens of life fall back on our shoulders for in reality we are driven by our wounds and the world's pressures, playing God, trying to survive. Nevertheless, God meets us, blesses us and grows us but it is despite us for we have our own agendas.

How different is life in the Waterfall. Here we do not hinder God's plan for us but our healing and equipping programme can unfold His way, in His time and at His speed as we are taken along in the Spirit's flow.

THE SANCTIFICATION PROCESS

WHEN WE ARE SAVED A PIECE OF US COMES UNDER THE LORDSHIP OF CHRIST

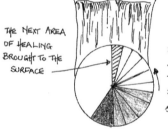

THE NEXT AREA OF HEALING BROUGHT TO THE SURFACE

IN THE WATERFALL IN THE FLOW OF THE SPIRIT, ALIGNED TO THE WILL OF THE FATHER, THE PROCESS SPEEDS UP.

24|7 WE WORK FOR THE LIVING GOD
24|7 WE ARE BEING TRANSFORMED
24|7 WE ARE BEING HEALED

PIECE BY PIECE WE ARE TRANSFORMED INTO THE LIKENESS OF CHRIST

It is the Sanctification process. When we give our life to Christ He comes in and is Lord over a piece of us that He will never relinquish.

Then little by little as we move on with Him He brings the next wedge under His Lordship. When we come into the Waterfall the process can speed up because now we are working with God and not for ourselves.

Here in this place there is not a minute of the day when we are not serving the Living God because we are aligned to His will and purpose. This is 'THE PLACE...'

> *... where everything works for good for those who love the Lord and SERVE HIS PURPOSE. Romans 8:28*

Jesus died on the Cross so our broken image can be restored, so that we can be healed from the inside out and return to the environment where we were designed to live, in the presence of the Father. In the Waterfall of His love as we say in trust *"I'll follow you."* God can do what needs to be done with our co-operation. Things are speeded up. God can now bring into being His plan for our healing and equipping, to prepare us to do for the Kingdom all He has destined us to accomplish.

> *For we are God's handiwork, created in Christ Jesus to do good works, which God prepared in advance for us to do. Ephesians 2:10*

GOD'S PERSPECTIVE OF YOU

If you are going to live in the Waterfall you have to believe what God says about you. This is very hard for us and we are going to explore why this is so later. At this stage let us say it is because of what is going on inside us, our judgement of our unworthiness makes it hard for us to believe what God says about us. HOWEVER, this again is about who God is much more than about us. What God says in His Word is true. If you say, *"Well it's true for you but He cannot mean it about me. I'm not good enough."* you are in effect saying that God is a liar, that the sacrifice of Jesus on the cross was not good enough for you and the Bible needs to be edited on the basis of your unworthiness.

Our beginning to learn the truth of who we are is the first stage of the renewing of our minds, turning from the distortions of worldly thinking and back to the health of Godly thinking. To begin we need to decide to believe what the Word says:

> *Therefore, I urge you, brothers and sisters, in view of God's mercy, to offer your bodies as a living sacrifice, holy and pleasing to God – this is your true and proper worship. Do not conform to the pattern of this world, but be transformed by the renewing of your mind. Then you will be able to test and approve what God's will is – his good, pleasing and perfect will.*
> *Romans 12:1-2*

NOTES

_____

_____

_____

_____

_____

YOU BELONG AND ARE UNCONDITIONALLY LOVED

We are going to look later at what blocks us from eating and being nourished by what God says about us. However, it is a good habit to begin to read the Word and apply it to yourself.

God cannot lie; He cannot act outside His character. What is in the Bible is THE TRUTH, so in faith believe. This is a decision you make and has nothing to do with the way you feel about yourself.

He loves you and you belong to Him. You are not a mistake. He created you uniquely to be who you are. At this moment you may be unaware of how amazing you are because you are too wounded to see your own beauty, yet that does not negate what God says.

ACTIVITY

1. Read Psalm 139
2. Read the Father's love letter – in the Appendix
3. To see how the Father feels about you read the Parable of the Lost Son in Luke 15:11-31

You may find it helpful to record your reflections.

YOU ARE VALUED AND HAVE WORTH

Do you know that if there were scales in front of the Father now and you were on one side and Jesus was on the other THEY WOULD BALANCE because in the Father's eyes you have the same value as Jesus Christ? If not, the Cross would not have saved us. You can only redeem a treasure by exchanging it with something of the same value. We are a royal priesthood. We belong to the family of the Living God, we are the sons and daughters of the King. How differently do we experience life when we believe these truths.

YOUR LIFE HAS MEANING and PURPOSE

As you live in the Waterfall because you have aligned yourself to the will of God, there is not a minute of the day when you are not serving His purposes. God's plan is for Jesus to return and for His church to be both His bride, pure and holy and His army, fit for battle. He is preparing you for the role that only you can play in this story. Thus the Waterfall Journey has Kingdom significance for each of us. God does not want us to be doing good things but to be doing the right thing, at the right time for His master plan. As we follow Him, He will lead us to be everything He designed us to be and do. The confirmation of this is in Psalms:

The Lord will fulfil His purpose for me. Psalm 138:8

Jesus is our supreme example of how to live in the Waterfall. He never strived or rushed. He stayed close to His Father: listening, *"speaking the words the Father gave Him to say"*; obeying, *"doing the things the Father gave Him to do"* and working when the Holy Spirit was upon Him. He achieved all that His Father set before Him. However, over forty times in the Gospels Jesus withdrew to be refreshed and replenished before continuing His mission. He abided in the presence of the Father where the peace that the world cannot know is to be found.

**HOW DO I DO THAT? –
GET INTO THE WATERFALL**
The good news is the Waterfall is only ever a step away.

- **I CAN CHOOSE** to live in the Waterfall of God's love. It is a decision I can make because Jesus has opened up the way. I can step into the Father's presence.
- **I CAN REPENT** of living my life my way, independently from God.
- **I CAN DECLARE** from this time I choose to trust God in every aspect of my life.
- **I CAN STEP** through the Cross and be cleansed of my sin by the blood of Jesus and stand in the Waterfall.
- **I CAN LIVE** in the presence of the Father, back in the spiritual heart to heart communication that was lost in the Fall and IF I TAKE BACK CONTROL OF MY LIFE I CAN BE FORGIVEN AGAIN.

THE KEY IS SELF-AWARENESS. When we find ourselves with our bucket at the well, looking for love or approval or trying to make ourselves feel okay or trying to fill the emptiness inside, we are sinning. What is in our bucket becomes our idol in place of what we should be drawing from our relationship with the Father. Acknowledging the sin means:

WE CAN REPENT and we can turn back. Jesus by His payment of the price for our sin has opened the way to give us access back into the Waterfall to stand in the Father's presence.

FORGIVEN AND CLEANSED by the blood of Jesus we can live in the relationship the Father intended us to enjoy and work 24/7 for the living God.

IF WE TAKE BACK CONTROL WE CAN REPENT AGAIN. As we have lived in the fallen world for so long, our habits are entrenched in playing god and being independent but we can be forgiven as many times as it takes to establish our life in the Waterfall.

I learned to wake in the morning and declare, "I choose to live in the Waterfall today." I would abide in the presence of the Father. Often I would find that I had wrestled back control from Him and was busy doing what I thought was best.

Becoming aware of this, I would STOP, look at the bucket in my cistern and what I was doing, repent by saying sorry and turn.

I pictured moving from the well through the Cross, receiving forgiveness and being cleansed, and in freedom I would step into the Waterfall.

I would raise my hands over my head and imagine standing in the flow of the Father's love for me which would pour over me and through me and I would state, "I trust you Lord". Some days I would be doing this many times but gradually I learned the difference between life in and out of the Waterfall. My desire to be home with the Father grew and I would hate moving out of His presence. I think this awareness was heightened for me because I was very aware of what life had been like in the dark years when I had shut God out of my life.

REFLECTION

Spend some time reflecting on where you are on your journey NOW.

Jesus beckons, *"Come and see."*

The Father awaits.

The CHOICE is yours.

NOTES

PART TWO

RESTORING THE BROKEN IMAGE

INTRODUCTION
We are going to explore the pain that distorts the created image we were born to be, so that we can be aware of what is going on within us and co-operate with the Holy Spirit in our healing.

However there is a HEALTH WARNING:
It is the ministry of the Holy Spirit to lead us on our journey of healing. We do not want to go racing ahead of Him; He knows what, when and how and so it is important that we do not dig for issues but wait until they surface. The purpose of these chapters is to make you aware of the process of healing and help you to be open to the Holy Spirit's leading.
If you are going to do the exercises, or issues begin to surface, you may want to talk through your experience with a trusted spiritual companion.

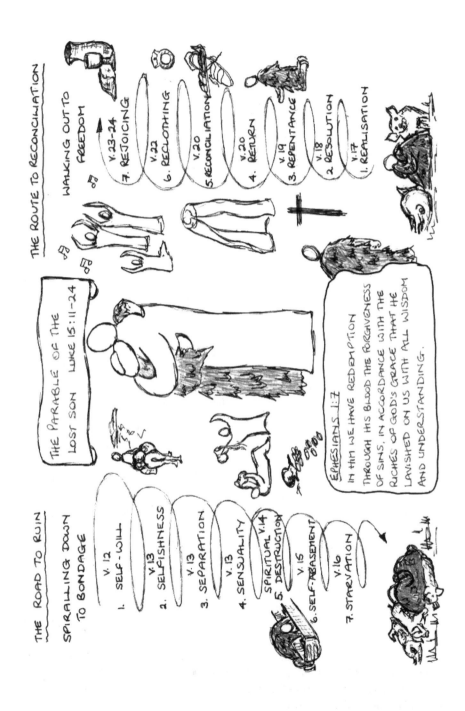

THE ROUTE TO RECONCILIATION

WALKING OUT TO FREEDOM

7. REJOICING — V.23-24
6. RECLOTHING — V.22
5. RECONCILIATION — V.20
4. RETURN — V.20
3. REPENTANCE — V.19
2. RESOLUTION — V.18
1. REALISATION — V.17

THE PARABLE OF THE LOST SON   LUKE 15:11-24

EPHESIANS 1:7
IN HIM WE HAVE REDEMPTION THROUGH HIS BLOOD THE FORGIVENESS OF SINS, IN ACCORDANCE WITH THE RICHES OF GOD'S GRACE THAT HE LAVISHED ON US WITH ALL WISDOM AND UNDERSTANDING.

THE ROAD TO RUIN

SPIRALLING DOWN TO BONDAGE

1. SELF-WILL — V.12
2. SELFISHNESS — V.13
3. SEPARATION — V.13
4. SENSUALITY — V.13
5. SPIRITUAL DESTRUCTION — V.14
6. SELF-ABASEMENT — V.15
7. STARVATION — V.16

CHAPTER 4

THE PROBLEM OF PAIN

*Let anyone who is thirsty come to me and drink. Whoever, believes in me, as
Scripture has said, rivers of living water will flow from within them.*
John 7: 37

THE DISCIPLE AND PAIN

Our pain stops us from being who God created us to be. The truth is that there
were thousands of followers of Jesus but only twelve disciples. Today most of the
followers of Jesus are stuck in their silent pain and only a few are willing to face the
injuries of their past. If we are going to be the army of the King we are hampered by
having most of the army on the sick list.

On the Waterfall Journey the elements, our growth to maturity, our calling and
equipping, the process of our healing are an interwoven fabric. When we come to
know Jesus the sanctification process begins, piece by piece God heals us and brings
us under His Lordship. When we commit to Waterfall living He can speed up that
process as we, in the flow of the Spirit, co-operate with Him. God knows not only
how to heal us but when and in what order. We are not in the business of digging up
wounds but of understanding when He puts His finger on the next aspect He wants
to work on in us, how we can co-operate with the Holy Spirit.

The process of our healing is part of our equipping. How we experience this and
how we see and understand the unfolding picture will help us walk beside others
in God's time. As we learn what God is doing in us, our self awareness and our
involvement in God's purposes speed up and clarity comes through finding God's
perspectives. Thus, our healing is essential for our progress towards wholeness and
maturity.

God paid a high price for our opportunity to be whole and healed and back in His
presence. Physical miracles make headlines but over the years I have seen many
healing miracles as God has cured emotional wounds which have contorted the
image and devastated a person's life.

WE ALL HAVE PAIN

In a previous chapter we have seen that we were born to live in the conditions and relationships that were spoken of in Genesis 1 & 2. Just as for a fish the natural life-giving habitat is water, so living in the presence of the Father is where we were created to live. We NEED the River of Water of Life which flows from the throne of heaven. After the Fall and cut off from that sustaining relationship, the fish were out of the water! We were on the bank of the river gasping, thirsting, empty and it hurt.

God created us with free will because His life force is and was and ever shall be, love. Therefore, we as His children have the power to make choices. The choice made in the Garden had a brutal outcome for all of us.

 Pain entered the world through the Fall. The forbidden fruit promised the belief that Adam and Eve would know right from wrong: that they would be able to make their own judgements, order their own world and live independently of the Father.

However, the unlooked for consequences of disobedience and sin were immediate and drastic. As soon as they ate the fruit:

They realised they were naked: so they sewed fig leaves together and made coverings for themselves. Genesis 3:7

Then they heard the sound of God coming for His customary walk with them, in the cool of the day and to His query, "Where are you?", Adam replied:

I heard you in the garden and I was afraid because I was naked: so I hid. Genesis 3:10

The consequences were literally shattering. They were instantly afraid of the Father, love and trust were replaced by fear and shame. In turn these previously unknown feelings drove them to new types of reactions. Ashamed, they did what they could to hide their nakedness; afraid, they ran from and hid from the source of their life.

In anger and guilt they turned on each other as God spoke further:

And He said, "Who told you that you were naked? Have you eaten from the tree that I commanded you not to eat from?" The man said, "The woman you put here with me – she gave me some fruit from the tree and I ate it." Genesis 3:11-12

In a dawning sense of loss Adam tried to jettison the responsibility for his actions first on God and then on Eve and she immediately shifted the responsibility and blame onto the serpent:

Then the Lord God said to the woman, "What is this you have done?" The woman said, "The serpent deceived me, and I ate." Genesis 3: 13

The consequences of their actions were unstoppable. Now desolate, each in thirst and in a new isolation they were evicted from Eden, for sin is sin and it cannot remain in the presence of the Father. The easy heart to heart, spirit to spirit flow of love and understanding, through which the infilling of their hearts was sustained was lost; perfection was marred. Thus our image, which required the fullness of the relationship with the Father to flourish, was now destined to be distorted by pain and hardship. The extent of the fall from grace can be seen in the contrast between Chapters 1& 2 of Genesis and Chapter 4 in which by verse 8 Cain murdered his brother, motivated by anger and jealousy.

LOVE IS THE FUEL

God's design was for us to be in families, with each partner drawing from their intimate relationship with the Father in the Waterfall, a constant overwhelming, surging, infilling of love to fuel their earthly relationships. Our God has a father's heart and a mother's heart for both give different aspects of love to us. This is mirrored in the earthly family, as fathers and mothers each give their children the same characteristics, which are essential to health, development and wellbeing.

A child should receive:

From the love of a father:
unconditional acceptance
unconditional love
security
significance

From the love of a mother:
unconditional acceptance
unconditional love
nurture
comfort

We are designed to be parents who, having a surfeit of love for each other, pour that love into our children, filling their hearts. The love of a father helps us build a clear sense of identity, to know our worth, in a safe and welcoming place. The love of the mother connects us to the place of belonging and holding. This models the love of God to our children until they are old enough to develop their own relationship with the Father in the Waterfall.

After the Fall no parents were going to be perfect, for the environment was not perfect. Children survive on what the parents can spare out of a dearth of love, not out of an overflowing. Parents do not have brimming over hearts because their parents did not and so it goes back. All of us have thirsts and emptiness. Yet we KNOW we are born to be filled with love and because our hearts are not filled with love they will be filled with anger. There are many cross babies about.

Whether we are aware of it or not, all of us have a well of pain within us.

OUTSIDE THE WATERFALL
THERE IS LESS LOVE THAN WE NEED

LOVE FLOWING FROM THE
FATHER'S HEART

IN THIS PLACE OF SECURITY
HEARTS ARE FILLED IN THE
FLOW OF LOVE

AS A CHILD TO
THE EXTENT THE HEART
IS NOT FILLED WITH LOVE
IT WILL BE FILLED WITH
ANGER.

I started counselling within a week of my dramatic conversion as I knew I needed 'to sort my head out'. On one level I knew I was in a very unhappy and hopeless place but I had no real self-awareness. I felt no pain and had no vocabulary of pain. On the first meeting with the counsellor I described myself as a cheerful and happy person despite all the evidence to the contrary.

Over many years of counselling I came to understand my story. When I was twenty-two months old on a visit to my grandparents I fell through a bedroom window, missing a rockery because I fell across a washing line, which bounced me beyond and onto the grass. I fractured my skull.

Things were different in the 1940s and in the hospital I was on my own in a darkened room, strapped down and my parents were not allowed in to see me. Abruptly I had been cut off from the flow of love that had been mine.

Not many years ago, over a period of three weeks the Holy Spirit took me through the physical pain experienced by me as a little person in the cot with a fractured skull. It is hard to find words to describe how bad it was. I do not know how I survived. It was like being scoured out inside. I was a Somme battlefield, all blasted devastation, no life to be seen and no colour, just shades of grey and black. Six weeks later I was discharged physically healed but emotionally shattered.

On the one occasion my Mum and Dad were brought into the room I reacted by screaming and pulling against the restraints. The doctor turned them around and walked them out. The message I received was 'big people cannot stand pain'. If you show it, you are abandoned again. Through the experience my trust in big people was obliterated and as an angry little person I made a vow to abandon the world. That decision underpinned my life for the next fifty years.

The little person that came out of hospital was very different to the one who went in. I had picked up beliefs about myself because of what I had experienced but little people are very subjective in what they understand. I came out believing I was unloved because otherwise why would Mum and Dad leave me hurting and in pain? The baby had no way of understanding the pain of Mum and Dad or of knowing of Mum's vigil outside the door. The hurt was so great that I tried to protect myself from pain by getting in first and abandoning the world. This was self-defeating, of course, because I then could not receive love; it could not penetrate the wall of disbelief I clothed myself in.

Our belief system drives the way we behave, so having learned that big people cannot stand pain I could not cry or show pain in case I was abandoned again. I survived by being cheerful. When hurt and bloodied in childhood emergencies I would spring up smiling. The conflict of beliefs I learned as a child boiled down to a fear of not being loved and knowing that I was unlovable. Panic and shame flowed round this immovable rock at the centre of my being; I KNEW there was something deeply wrong with me. Smothering the pain and acting a part to hide this truth became my unconscious response to life.

Once we have a belief in our minds, we are not going to let it go and we will hoover up evidence as we go through life to confirm our twisted beliefs about ourselves. We are very complex and there are consequences. Making life decisions on the basis of what I believed caused me to be a victim, a ricocheting cannonball, leaving a trail of damage behind me until I came to the end of me.

This accident was the mustard seed that led me to a mighty tree of trouble in the years that followed despite the motivation for all involved at that time being to see me well again. It is important to realise that much of the damage caused to us is unintentional: most parents do their best and many others have an input into our early lives, with circumstances and environment playing their part too. For the little person every experience is adding to their belief system.

GOD'S VIEW OF PAIN

God's view of pain is very different to ours. It was not part of life in the Garden of Eden but when it became part of life after the Fall, God was there for His people in their pain. The Psalms of David speak of God's compassion and involvement in all the suffering of mankind and it was His desire that we should look to Him for help. The Father sent Jesus to die for us so that we could be healed, He gave us the Holy Spirit as our Counsellor. All the resources of our creative, loving, powerful God are at our disposal for the restoration of each one of us to the image that we were created to be. Being the God He is, He then uses that pain as a resource for the kingdom, transforming our suffering, collecting our tears, *"restoring the years the locusts have eaten"*. My testimony is that He has transformed fifty years of pain into treasures for the Kingdom that bless me daily. He has healed my past and now I use that experience in my ministry. I often say, without any glibness, that I would go again through those fifty years to be where I am today, still a work in progress, but in such a relationship with God as to make it all worthwhile.

PETER'S STORY

 In trying to make sense of God's view of pain for others, the Holy Spirit showed me that the life of Peter can teach us some valuable lessons. We are introduced to him in Luke 5:1 – 10.

Just picture the scene, a group of tired and despondent fishermen were mending their nets after a fruitless night out fishing, when Jesus arrived on the beach surrounded by a large crowd. Peter must have been interested but he was about to be involved for Jesus asked if He might speak to the crowd from the fisherman's boat. Instead of heading off home and to bed Peter agreed and then he was a captive audience as Jesus ministered to the crowd.

What did Peter see in Jesus during that time? It was enough that when afterwards Jesus, the master carpenter said to him, the master fisherman,

> *"Go out and put down your net for a catch." Peter replied, "Because you say so I will do it." Luke 5:4*

This was remarkable for what Jesus was proposing went against all the knowledge and experience of the fisherman. Peter knew when it was best to catch fish and that was when he had been out on the lake. Now was not the time but because Jesus said go, he did it. On his return to the shore with the astonishing catch he was in awe, for he knew the natural world had been impacted by something that was supernatural and holy. He sank to his knees and said, *"Go away from me Lord, I am sinful man."*

However, Jesus had come that day to find His team. He had come for four men on that beach amongst the thousands, so Jesus looked Peter in the eye and said,

> *"Don't be afraid; from now on you will fish for people." So they pulled their boats up on the shore, left everything and followed him. Luke 5 : 10*

How astonishing! Might our response to Jesus be as wholehearted and total as that of Peter?

From reflection on this passage, the Holy Spirit revealed that Peter's life fell into three sections. There was the time before that moment on the beach; there were the three years Peter walked alongside Jesus; and there was the time after Pentecost when Peter took off into the full power of his ministry. This mirrors the pattern of our spiritual life.

Peter was an ordinary man, going through life doing his best with what was set before him. He had a family and lived in Capernaum which had the synagogue at its heart and was a vibrant community. He was a master fisherman running a fishing business with his partners. An ordinary man, born as we are into the fallen world, bruised and battered by life but moving forward as best he might. And then Jesus came.

Jesus set before Peter a line drawn in the sand on the beach. On one side stood Peter's known world, on the other side a great unknown. On one side the God as He was known in the synagogue, family responsibilities, the needs of a business, relationships, dreams, expectations and competences. On the other side Jesus and a crazy adventure where nothing was known. Peter did not know what the job was, where he would sleep that night, what the future held, how he would provide for his family, nothing was known.

What he did know, through those first few hours with Jesus, was that he could trust Jesus completely for the things that concerned him. He knew in his heart that he wanted to respond with total commitment to the invitation in Jesus' eyes. Peter, when he crossed that line on the beach, stepped into the Waterfall aligning himself irrevocably with the will and purposes of God.

What a wonderful example of total faith in Jesus:

So they pulled their boats up on the shore, left everything and followed him.
Luke 5:11

The tourist boats on Lake Galilee today are replicas of a 2000 year old
wreck discovered at the bottom of the lake known as 'The Jesus Boat'.

There followed the second stage of his life, the years of discipleship. Constantly in company with Jesus, Peter was transformed from the inside out. He learned from the Master; he was healed and disciplined; he was involved with Jesus in every facet of that time from the large to the small; he learned the perspectives of God and the mind of Christ. He travelled, ate, relaxed and was refreshed in the presence of Jesus. He followed in trust. Notwithstanding these experiences, he made mistakes. He abandoned Jesus when it mattered but was forgiven and restored. Jesus foretold it:

Simon, Simon, Satan has asked to sift all of you as wheat. But I have prayed
for you, Simon, that your faith may not fail. And when you turn back,
strengthen your brothers. Luke : 31 – 32

He went on to betray Jesus after His arrest, denying three times that he knew Jesus. However, after the Resurrection, Peter was restored as he made his threefold affirmation of love to Jesus, again on a beach and surrounded by fish.

Then he was ready. When the Holy Spirit fell on him on the day of Pentecost Peter flowed into his full ministry. As the Rock on which the church was built his life affects all of us today. An ordinary man became extraordinary because he followed Jesus into the Waterfall.

So what about us? If the three part pattern is relevant to us what does it mean? In the years I have worked helping people to come into the Waterfall to learn how to live God's way and to become true disciples I now believe it is true for all of us.

We are all born into the fallen world and suffer emotional wounds and damage. God tells us that we each are travelling a known path:

> My frame was not hidden from you when I was made in the secret place, when I was woven together in the depths of the earth. Your eyes saw my unformed body; All the days ordained for me were written in your book before one of them came to be. Psalm 139: 15 – 16

This means the family you were born into and the events of your life have not been accidental. That is pretty hard to hear for some people. God has trusted some people with very hard journeys.

However, at some point there is the possibility of a change of season. The timing of this depends on what God has for you to do in stage three of your life. When you have all the necessary experiences for God to transform, you have your moment on the beach. This is not necessarily when you give your life to Christ but is the time and place where the decision is made to be a disciple and to totally align yourself to God's way. To trust Him for your family, for your security, and for your future, putting yourself and your life at His disposal, thus joining Him in His story and letting Him direct the part you will play in it.

My observation is that the season often changes when a person has a crisis and needs help. I always believe that those whom God sends to me are in that place and that their emotional turmoil is the signal for them to understand how their story can be redeemed in His. As their story unfolds there is a choice to take a risk and move into the Waterfall and let God be God in their life or to go on as before.

If they make a decision to trust God and live as He intended, the next stage begins and everything changes as radically as it did for Peter on the beach, for now essentially it is about learning to live intimately with God. They move into a new relationship with each person of the Trinity and the process of restoration and renewal, which began when they gave their life to Christ, can now be speeded up. Creatively, God transforms the pain of the past into His resources for ministry. When they are ready, sufficiently healed and restored, in God's time He will launch them into their full ministry which, because they have learnt to operate under His direction, will be effective in Kingdom terms.

WE ARE ALL ON A UNIQUE PATH

It is essential that we do not try and compare our walk with that of someone else. Comparisons tend towards "I have had more pain than you." or "Your journey was worse than mine." Judgements too, about the relative spirituality of the journey of an individual or yourself are missing the point and divisive. Does understanding that takes years to acquire means someone is less spiritual than those who learn early in life? No, we all have unique journeys depending what full ministry God has for us.

Let me just clarify what I mean by our full ministry by looking again at Peter's life. He did many significant things as he walked alongside Jesus. Sharing the ministry of those three years he was also being changed, healed and equipped. However, he stepped into full power and significance in God's story in the third stage of his life after Pentecost. In that third period of his life he fulfilled the unique ministry that only he could do. We all have full ministries waiting for us when we are ready.

Ideally, as people are saved and taught the fundamental God truths we are sharing then all believers would see there is a Waterfall to step into and the reality and the consequences of the choice set before them. At the moment, we fall short of this in the broad church maybe only because people do not understand the progression, being recruited into the army seems enough. However, the reality is that crossing the line on the beach and stepping into the Waterfall was only the start for Peter and so for us, of true discipleship. We need to teach the onward steps, just being in the Kingdom is not enough, the journey needs to continue for people to come into the richness of all that Jesus died to return to us.

Our lives are the learning ground for our full ministries. Whatever you have been through, God can turn it around. No wound or tear or experience is wasted if we are willing to let God deal with the pain. Unfortunately, many Christians, leaders and congregations will not go there.

Emotional pain that comes to the surface is God's red flag in the minefield saying, *"There is pain buried here and it is time to deal with it."* Residual pain blocks the restoration of our image and the work of the Kingdom. And right now, even as Peter the fisherman had no idea that he was to be a disciple of the Son of God and of his extraordinary destiny, you also may not have an idea of your full ministry. I bet you are thinking far too small. Who God reveals Himself to is a mystery but if you are reading this I can tell you he is either calling you in or inviting you higher. Standing still is not an option in discipleship. He wants to deal with your pain.

CHAPTER 5

UNDERSTANDING OURSELVES

In order to co-operate fully in our healing it helps to know how we were designed to function in Spirit-to-Spirit harmony with our Father. This diagram shows the Water of Life thundering through us as pure unblocked channels for where the love of the Father flows it brings life. Adam and Eve were such channels before the Fall.

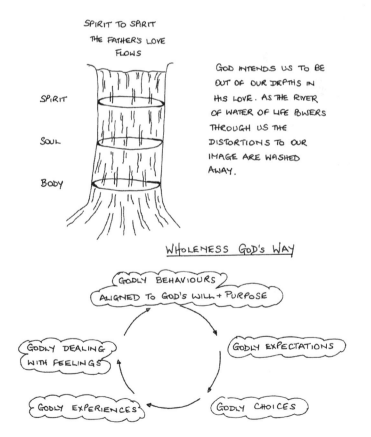

SPIRIT TO SPIRIT
THE FATHER'S LOVE
FLOWS

GOD INTENDS US TO BE OUT OF OUR DEPTHS IN HIS LOVE. AS THE RIVER OF WATER OF LIFE POWERS THROUGH US THE DISTORTIONS TO OUR IMAGE ARE WASHED AWAY.

SPIRIT

SOUL

BODY

WHOLENESS GOD'S WAY

GODLY BEHAVIOURS ALIGNED TO GOD'S WILL + PURPOSE

GODLY DEALING WITH FEELINGS

GODLY EXPECTATIONS

GODLY EXPERIENCES

GODLY CHOICES

However, as a result of the Fall there was a fundamental shift. The design of mankind was literally turned on its head. Self and worldly considerations came to the surface and the spiritual life of man became sidelined. The diagram 'Understanding our broken image' more accurately represents how we now function and can be very useful as we try to understand our own stories.

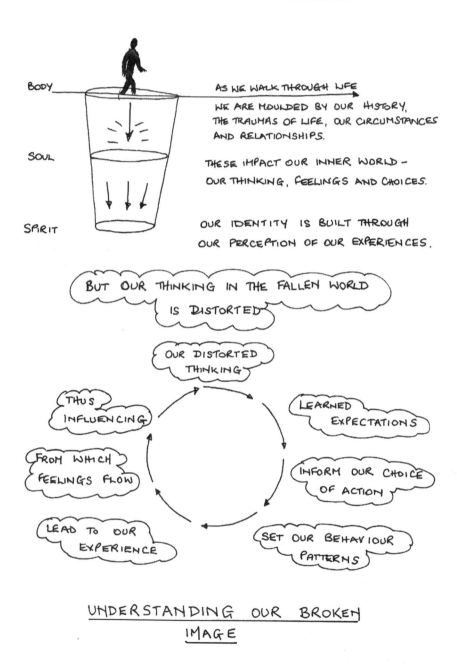

BODY

AS WE WALK THROUGH LIFE

WE ARE MOULDED BY OUR HISTORY, THE TRAUMAS OF LIFE, OUR CIRCUMSTANCES AND RELATIONSHIPS.

SOUL

THESE IMPACT OUR INNER WORLD – OUR THINKING, FEELINGS AND CHOICES.

SPIRIT

OUR IDENTITY IS BUILT THROUGH OUR PERCEPTION OF OUR EXPERIENCES.

BUT OUR THINKING IN THE FALLEN WORLD IS DISTORTED

OUR DISTORTED THINKING

THUS INFLUENCING

LEARNED EXPECTATIONS

FROM WHICH FEELINGS FLOW

INFORM OUR CHOICE OF ACTION

LEAD TO OUR EXPERIENCE

SET OUR BEHAVIOUR PATTERNS

UNDERSTANDING OUR BROKEN IMAGE

We have a bodily form and we physically walk through the days of our life with events and experiences shaping us. These feed an inner story where we translate the happenings into our beliefs which affect our choices and result in our feelings. We then use this evidence to wrap ourselves in an identity which rarely is the image God created us to be but more what we think the world says we are.

BODY

The Body area depicts what we have experienced on the surface of our lives as we have walked out each day. It is our story. The first years have great significance as we pick up so many of our beliefs about ourselves at that time. It is also made up of the triumphs and disasters, the relationships and the circumstances we have enjoyed or endured.

Each of us has a shape to fill. We were created to always have defined borders, a space to occupy, a growing image as we come to maturity that is a sacred space where the Holy Spirit dwells. As we travel that image is buffeted and attacked from all sides and we become invaded and our borders can break down. There are many forms of abuse - emotional, psychological, physical and sexual and all of them are invasions across our borders. There are heart-rending programmes on the television that graphically expose the long lasting effects of such incursions. The truth is that none of us can get through life without damage whether we are aware of it or not.

The pivotal event in my life was the experience of those six weeks, in hospital at twenty-two months. That was the key to untwisting so many of the distortions that marred my image and made my experience of life so difficult thereafter. In the Fallen world all of us have been damaged in some way and have a broken and distorted image until restored by God's healing and truth.

The following exercise is illuminating. It is helpful just to review our journey and to reflect on the links and patterns of our lives as we will find insights there to light the path ahead. It also has great value when exploring an area of difficulty. I use it continually when helping people. Not only is it a revelation for an individual to see the cyclical patterns of their behaviour through life but it provides specific clues through the events that come to mind that enlighten the area being explored.

NOTES

ACTIVITY
DRAWING YOUR TIMELINE
Take a risk. Open yourself up to the Holy Spirit. As we go through this chapter I will suggest you do one or two things that will allow God to show you if He wants to do some work in you right now. Have courage; what God starts He will finish.

Drawing a timeline helps every time God embarks on a new work in you for it allows the Holy Spirit to throw up from your unconscious events He wants you to consider.

```
+ events
BIRTH -------------------------------------------------------NOW
- events
```

Taking no longer that 40 minutes plot the events that come into your mind in chronological order. Place positive events above and negative events below the line. Join the dots.
Ask the Holy Spirit to reveal to you anything He wants you to see.
Look for recurring patterns, links and influences.
Recording your findings can be very helpful

In our day-to-day walk through life every incident, every loss, every high and low point is significant because it feeds our inner world. It sets the way we characterise our life whether as a tragedy, a penal sentence, an endurance race, a fantasy, a comedy or a mystery.

FAMILY DYNAMICS

Sometimes it is the dynamic within our families that can be instrumental in setting the characteristics for us. It can happen where there is a relationship or situation within the family that needs to be managed. For example:-
- Where drugs, alcohol, violence or abuse are present.
- Where desperate circumstances like redundancy, chronic or mental illness, poverty, or long term unemployment are endured by the family.
- Perhaps the family has a 'star' performer in their midst, around whom the family life revolves.

In these families the individuals are likely to take on a particular role in the theatre of family life. It is just like a play and to survive and keep the plot moving each character acts out their designated part and just as in acting there is a script and rules that govern the play.

POSSIBLE ROLES FOUND IN FAMILY LIFE

THE CENTRAL ROLE – the power and interests of this person dominate the household. Their life may look commendable to the outside world, (for example it could be a high profile pastor) but a price may be paid in the home. The family may need to act out perfect family life to fulfil the illusion of perfect Christian living in order to sustain the image of the 'star'. The mood and behaviours of this all-powerful person will colour life for everyone else.

THE CHIEF ENABLER – this role is usually, but not exclusively, taken by an adult as they keep things running in the household. They are the peacekeeper, the financier, the carer, the preventer and the protector. The role combines constant attention to the situation NOW, galloping exhaustion and powerlessness to alter outcomes. However, it is this person who keeps and maintains the central person in their damaging behaviour. Why should they change when this person ensures that life hangs together?

THE LOST CHILD – takes the position as a junior enabler, trying to keep things calm and normal. Their needs are subsumed by the needs of the central character. They lose their childhood under a burden of responsibility for keeping the family safe and within the rules.

THE SCAPEGOAT – takes the blame, is always in trouble, cannot get it right. They are in the spotlight acting as a distraction from the real problem. Dumping blame on them is an easy way for everyone else to feel better.

THE HERO – brings pride into the family and is seen as good, a peacemaker. They seem to prove that all is right within the family.

THE CLOWN – reads and reacts to the tension, using humour to defuse and distract from darkness and difficulty. The mask hides the fear that things will be seen as they really are.

THE BLACK SHEEP – cannot conform to the family system. They rebel and distance themselves from the heart of the family, escaping as soon as they are able.

THE UNWRITTEN RULES OF FAMILY LIFE

Now the cast is assembled the actors obey a set of unbreakable, unwritten rules.

1. **SECRECY** – Not only must the problem be kept secret from those outside the family but within the home the pretence that the problem does not exist must be maintained. It can therefore never be spoken about or acknowledged.

2. **NO OUTSIDERS** – Visitors and friends are not welcome in case they see the truth. This is especially hard on the children as it isolates them from their peers but adults too will suffer from isolation.

3. **KEEP THE STATUS QUO** – It is essential that circumstances do not get out of control. Instability is dangerous for then the reality might come into view. Any disruption is dangerous and those who disrupt, such as the black sheep in not conforming or the scapegoat in getting it wrong, are reviled.

4. **THE NEEDS OF OTHERS ARE MORE IMPORTANT THAN YOUR OWN** – So all feelings must be suppressed. The feelings of others, especially the central character's feelings, influence all of life in the family. The rule is to trust no-one and to never show vulnerability. Typically, the actors find something to distract themselves from the pain and so bury themselves in school or work or chocolate.

4. **DENY YOURSELF** – The message is clear, the needs of the individual are unimportant. No-one is allowed to have fun or to play or be themselves.

My second husband Johnnie was an alcoholic. I had married him because one afternoon he was kind to me. I was so desperate for some love and gentleness that I ignored the evidence of what the reality of life with him would be like, which I well knew, having been a confidante of his previous wife, who died of cancer.

I was the Chief Enabler in our family system. My husband was medically retired and the shape of his days was to sleep most of the day, go drinking through the evening, requiring a meal around 11pm and then staying awake through the night. I had a full time job, two teenage children from my previous marriage and a difficult ex-husband. I did all the things that maintained the stability of Johnnie's regime and moods, manipulating everyone else to that end. I tried to protect my children and prevent earthquakes but my actions were allowing Johnnie to follow his unreasonable pattern of life. The children suffered because I was just trying to hold things together and so were they.

Such systems are addressed by disrupting the scheme of things so that the central person is confronted by the effects of their behaviour on others.

God created us for family life so that in a safe, harmonious and rich environment we would blossom and grow. We can see that when there are the difficulties we have been looking at, children especially cannot be themselves, their sense of identity gets lost and they become victims without power. The characteristics of the role we played within our family system can go with us into adult life and affect the next generation unless addressed. Just as actors need to de-role we may need to lay aside the part we played at home within our family.

REFLECTION

EXERCISE: The aim of this is to help us grow self-awareness and to unravel our experiences.

Think about one good major relationship of your childhood and do a spider diagram of significant events, both good and difficult, involving that person. This example is about my father.

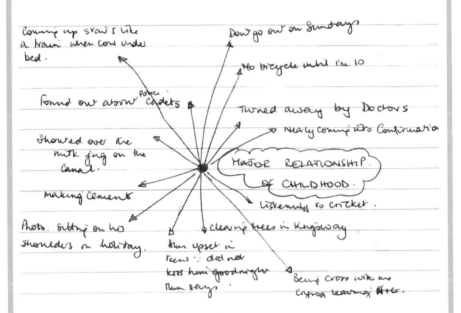

Then reflect on your relationship:-
- What feelings did you experience on each occasion?
- What effect did that have on the way you thought about yourself?
- What choices and behaviours did each event trigger for you?
- Then stand back from the detail and reflect on what this person has brought to your life as a whole.

Record your reflections.

NOTES

SOUL - OUR INNER STORY

BODY

AS WE WALK THROUGH LIFE
WE ARE MOULDED BY OUR HISTORY,
THE TRAUMAS OF LIFE, OUR CIRCUMSTANCES
AND RELATIONSHIPS.

SOUL

THESE IMPACT OUR INNER WORLD –
OUR THINKING, FEELINGS AND CHOICES.

SPIRIT

OUR IDENTITY IS BUILT THROUGH
OUR PERCEPTION OF OUR EXPERIENCES.

What we experience on the outside as we walk through life is informing our inner story, the soul area, which is made up of our belief system, the choices we make and the consequent feelings we experience. To begin to look at this inner domain we are going to explore the world of feelings.

BURIED PAIN

The circumstances of our life mould us. Our story begins before we are born for even as we are carried by our mother in the womb we are picking up messages. I worked with a lady, also a counsellor, who was mystified by having panic attacks whenever she experienced very sudden, loud noises. These had increased dramatically of late because some demolition and building work had commenced close to her home. She had received much emotional healing over the years but was baffled by where this reaction originated.

We discovered that when her mother was pregnant with her in the war there were nightly bombing raids on Bristol. The men were away and a group of young mothers were together in the neighbourhood bomb shelter night after night. Her mother was anxious and threatened and the explosions brought panic to them all as they tried to survive and keep their children safe. What her Mum experienced was buried within the unborn baby and the current noises triggered the fear and helplessness felt on those dangerous nights.

Everything we have ever experienced is filed away in our memories and each experience has feelings attached to it. We do not like pain so we learn very early in life to bury it but that is akin to burying a bag of ferrets. Feelings have life of their own and it takes a gym full of energy to keep them down in our unconscious. One of the reasons that we see many people with depression in their forties and fifties is that often they have just run out of the energy needed to keep the ferrets quiet.

God created us with feelings to enrich our lives but the reality for most of us seems very different. The problem is when we bury feelings we tend to bury all feelings for if you cannot feel pain you cannot feel joy. Being detached from our feelings we begin to act out a part, trying to get the love we crave and to feel okay about ourselves, yet we act out what we think others need to see. Thus the gap between the person we show to the outside world and the truth of what is within us grows wider as the years go by. How different was the example of Jesus. He was authentic. He acknowledged and owned His feelings and expressed them; there was a true connection between His inner world and His response to the outward circumstances of His life.

We have many taboos about feelings that exacerbate the damage of emotional injury, for example expecting that 'big boys don't cry'. Also often we just want the other person to be okay because we cannot stand to see their pain, therefore we will close down the space for them to expose their grief. Loss is a part of the rhythm of everyday life, grieving is a natural process and children need to do it too. This is rarely understood by big people. One of my friends who lost her father when she was seven spent the whole of her childhood in a depressed state. It was only when she was doing her counselling training that she understood that she had never grieved for the loss of her father because the big people around her at the time were unaware of her need to do so.

Even with adults we can be very impatient. Often after a few months we feel those who have lost partners should be getting over it. In reality it can be five years before the grieving process is completed. We do not want to hear if people are in pain and we dare not share our pain, for then people would know the truth about us. So "I'm fine" is the biggest and most frequent lie spoken out in churches today.

It means <u>F</u>eelings <u>I</u>nside <u>N</u>ot <u>E</u>xpressed.

Now in counselling and beginning to explore my story I began to be aware of something inside me that was beyond words. The Holy Spirit took a hand. I was in town and when passing an Early Learning Centre I felt compelled to go inside. I wandered around and then stood transfixed. I was looking at a grizzly bear.

I was overwhelmed by something inside me that I could not describe. What I could see was a bear backed into a cave, covered in sores, at the end of its tether, without hope. It was isolated and angry and was cut off from the world it inhabited.

I took it with me to counselling but for many sessions just held it. Gradually I began to be able to describe what was going on for the bear, though the feelings had nothing to do with me. After some time there was something else but it was not the bear. So then I went into the Early Learning Centre again and this time it was a gorilla that spoke. To me, the gorilla was all the sadness in the world but again the sadness was not mine. I could feel pity for the gorilla but could still turn away from owning the sadness.

Then my counsellor did a wonderful thing. He went to the Early Learning Centre and bought a bag of animals. For months after that, my therapy was playing with the animals. I would put a baby panda snuggled next to the feet of an elephant and would feel enormously comforted. The little panda surrounded by the lions and tigers spoke of my fears; when I felt hopeless, I would just stack the animals in a big pile and sit in silence. I acted out my feelings through them. It was many months and a huge leap forward when I managed to acknowledge those feelings as my own.

Those plastic animals were the bridge that allowed me to reconnect my outer shell with my inner story.

FEELINGS

We cannot choose our feelings; they are what they are but we can choose what we do with them. It would be great if when we were young we were taught about feelings because so many of us are completely unaware of what lurks inside us. This lack of knowing what is inside means we not only have no vocabulary to express what is going on for us but we shy away from any show of emotion by others. The truth is that understanding our feelings is a life skill that enhances our ability to form rich relationships.

NOTES

HOW DO I DO THAT –
DEAL WITH FEELINGS IN A HEALTHY WAY?

TUNE INTO YOUR FEELINGS
Begin to grow your awareness of what is going on within you.
Stop and ask yourself, "What do I feel?"
Reflect on circumstances, try and name the feelings they produce
in you.
Difficult feelings may be showing you that there is a wound waiting to
be healed.

OWN YOUR FEELINGS
Owning your feelings is key, no-one makes you feel.
Feelings are generated from triggers which resonate within you; for
example from a sight, a smell or a behaviour.
Not "You made me feel sad." but "I am sad." This is my sadness. We
need to take responsibility for our own feelings.

FEEL THEM
This allows you to deal with them now and not to bury a ticking time
bomb. We have learnt through life to run away from our feelings,
instead we need turn and walk into them.
Acknowledge how bad or good they are, stick with them.

EXPRESS THEM APPROPRIATELY
We are masters of off-loading our feelings onto others but we need to
take responsibility for their safe disposal. Find creative ways to let your
feelings flow in a safe way that does not damage others.
Choose how you respond, avoid reacting out of feelings.
Most of us have a bag of ferrets of pain and difficult feelings buried
within us but it is finite; they can be released.

DEAL WITH ANY ISSUES RAISED
When you have let the energy of your feelings go, you can bring
your mind to bear on what was going on for you, what triggered the
feelings and deal with the issues exposed.

DEALING WITH PAIN TAKES COURAGE
We dislike to see people in pain. We tend to try and make things
better for them. God's view is different. He wants to release pain
because it surrounds the site of a hidden wound that needs to be
uncovered to be healed.

As my counselling progressed I became aware of the burden of pain I was carrying from the cot in the hospital. I was astounded that I had managed to get through life at all. The fear of feeling had continually consumed of my internal resources and with the energy needed to keep the 'ferrets' of buried feelings quiet, it was no wonder I had become exhausted and imploded that evening in Glasgow.

Now I understood much of where the feelings came from and I was acknowledging and owning them but what to do with them? To be honest I was terrified because I realised all that had ever driven me was pain and if I gave up the pain inside me what would be left ? Who would I be?

As I work now with others I know this is a real sticking point. At some point we need to take a risk and choose life. Feeling the terror, I reflected on the Waterfall and looked at the choices . They were pretty stark. Either keep the pain and all the anguish and hurt that had flowed out of my damage or take the risk, step out and trust God for healing.

I declared to God that I chose to be healed and receive the healing that Jesus died to make possible. Nothing happened.

Some days later I was sitting quietly when the intensity of the feelings I had discovered were present in the cot overwhelmed me: the fear, the loss, the puzzlement, the despair, the isolation, the blackness, the physical pain. I was back there with the wounds uncovered. It was then I saw that Jesus was standing beside the cot and He picked me up and held me.

I learnt a big lesson that day. It is not that we just have to feel the feelings but we have to follow the feelings back to their source like a hound following the scent of a fox back to its den. The source of the original wound is where the healing is needed. So if we stop ourselves or others exploring feelings, if we try to make people feel better, we close down the opportunity for God to heal the root of the problem. However, this needs to be under the direction of the Holy Spirit.

I now know too, that God can heal in layers. He knows the depth to go to at a particular moment that is right for each of us. I know now that God can heal emotional hurts in an instant or through a process. The way He heals in each particular instance is part of our equipping, for it is with the comfort we receive that we will comfort others.

Jesus held me. Now I knew that He was always there at the cot and healing came, for there was a purpose. I was not outside His care and I could trust Him to turn it to good.

However, it felt there was a dam within me behind which all these feelings were piled up. Over the next few weeks I spoke in counselling about there being cracks in the dam and leaks down the face of it. I was scared of what might happen if or when the dam crumbled and held on to these verses reminding God that He could not break His word:

Fear not, for I have redeemed you; I have summoned you by name; you are mine. When you pass through the waters, I will be with you; and when you pass through the rivers they will not sweep over you. When you walk through the fire you will not be burned; the flames will not set you ablaze. Isaiah 43:1-2

Again I was at rest when the dam broke. I saw it give way and a wall of filthy water was released. I remember feeling horror at what was in the water but watched it go through steep gorges and down a valley and out onto an open plain. There it spread out and watered the land. Then, as I watched, the ground changed from hard and infertile to green and beautiful, cloaked in wild flowers. What swept over me was enormous relief.

Then I stood in the Waterfall and let that crystal river of the clear pure water of life flow in me and through me washing away the stench and horrors of the filthy waters from the dam. I saw the water flowing through from my head, through my body and out of my limbs filling me with light and lightness and thus healing came.

That pain had been transformed to become the foundation out of which my ministry now flows.

It takes courage to listen to others in pain. It takes courage to be vulnerable in our own pain. The journey to being able to drop the pretence that we are okay, to stop playing a role, to be authentic and transparent as Jesus modelled, is the journey to wholeness and is essential for all disciples.

DIFFICULT FEELINGS

Understanding something of the particular feelings that cause us difficulty and what they mean in terms of our story can help us as we co-operate with the Holy Spirit in our healing. Let's look at the difficult feelings we see generated in Genesis 3, which we looked at in Chapter 4: The Problem of Pain.

We are going to look at three classes of feelings that were immediately apparent after the Fall: anger, anxiety and shame. Each class is a continuum stretching from a small feeling through to shattering volumes of emotion. How much we feel is dependent on how important the issue that generates the emotion is to us.

ANGER

Anger is one of the biggest threats to relationships. As Adam and Eve sinned, immediately they were blaming the other and off-loading responsibility for their own actions. Anger smashed the unity and closeness they had enjoyed. From then on they had individual agendas. The seeds of violence and murder were now in the world.

Anger can stretch from slight irritation, which we can shake off, through to rage and fury, which can consume us. Always the goal of our behaviour is to reach the bucket in our cistern where we believe our idols will deliver our needs. Anger arises when we are blocked from that goal. Imagine a person who feels they must always look stunning in order to be okay. If someone spills a full cup of coffee down them just before they have a meeting their goal will be blocked and their temper will rise. The strength of the feeling gives us an indication of how important we believe the content of the bucket is to us. So if we are irritated it is a relatively minor matter but if we are enraged something pretty big is going down for us.

IRRITATION   ANGER   RAGE

Anger is one of the most uncomfortable feelings because it can be volcanic and can seem to come out of nowhere. Buried anger is the liveliest of ferrets and takes considerable energy to keep quiet. Often outbursts of rage trigger people to seek help because it is such a frightening, out of control experience. Also because anger is energy, to be on the receiving end of someone's fury can be very damaging, especially if it is being dumped on you. "You made me angry!" shouted up close to another person is psychologically intimidating and abusive and can feel like an assault.

When we are little we can only express anger in two ways, verbally or through our behaviour. Big people often shut down both these avenues for little people insisting on 'nice' behaviour. The destructive power of anger can be released by activity, shouting, digging, writing, and we will each have different ways that suit us. Ideally, every home would have an angry corner where all members of the household are free to go and bash a cushion, jump up and down and use bad language to get rid of the energy of anger. When that is safely defused the issue that is causing the anger can be addressed.

In society today, in homes and on the streets anger is defining life. Domestic and street violence and the blame culture may seem obvious examples but the use of drugs and self-harming are examples of how anger without expression can be turned inward with destructive energy.

Jesus was not frightened of being angry with the Pharisees and with the stall holders in the Temple. It was His anger and He owned it and took responsibility for its expression. As Christians we often believe it is wrong for us to be angry but I would say again we cannot choose our feelings, we need to own them and deal with them in a healthy way. Ephesians gives good advice:

In your anger do not sin: Do not let the sun go down while you are still angry, and do not give the devil a foothold. Ephesians 4:26

Anger is a helpful pointer to what is going on within us, for it is telling us that to our perception something is blocking our way to having our needs met.

ANXIETY

After eating the fruit and shattering the harmony of trust, Adam and Eve were afraid and hid when they heard God calling them. They no longer knew where their relationship with Him stood. Change and loss opened up for the first time in their lives the chasm of the unknown. They did not know if God's love was still theirs and their minds were full of questions to which they did not know the answer. What was going to happen to them? What was God going to do?

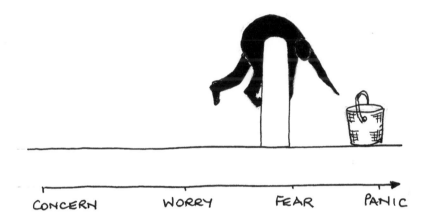

In the fallen world we experience anxiety when we are uncertain that we are going to be able to reach what we think we need in the bucket from our well. Will we get it or not?

Anxiety can stretch from slight concern at one end of the spectrum to galloping fear and panic at the other.

Fear is debilitating and robs us of being who we were created to be. It is no coincidence that continually we are told in the Bible, *"Fear not"* and *"Do not worry."* However, for most of us fear will play a part in our lives.

A baby is incredible at picking up impressions about the world it has come into and the top of the list of things to know is, "Am I safe?" and "Can I trust big people?" Sadly, because we are in the fallen world things are less than perfect. We should stress here that most parents are doing their best for their children and this is not a judgement on them. The less-than-perfect circumstances also play a considerable part in making little ones feel less than safe. Their anxiety comes from not knowing whether they are going to get their needs met.

A baby experiences love by the tone of voice used, the gentle touch, the firm holding, the look in the big person's eyes, being warm and dry and being fed. If there is major disruption to receiving consistent love and care, the feeling of safety for the little one will be compromised.

For whatever reason, if we have experienced this, we will develop strategies to try to keep ourselves safe. One common way is to try to control life, manipulating others and circumstances to conform to what we need. If people do not co-operate thus blocking our needs from being met, anger too will come and join the party.

A fearful child may when they are six or seven be labelled as shy. This is a 'behaviour strategy' to keep safe. Instead of moving out, taking risks, meeting others and expanding their world they hang back and shut down. As the child grows up, this inner life influences their behaviour, often restricting their choices as the world may be a fearful place for them.

GUILT AND SHAME

Guilt is about what we do and shame is about who we are. Adam and Eve were immediately aware of their nakedness after eating the fruit and shame overcame them. Prior to this, nakedness had been part of the freedom they enjoyed but now their own judgement brought humiliation upon themselves.

Shame stretches from embarrassment at one end of the spectrum through to feeling a suicidal failure at the other. Shame means that I do not believe I am good enough to have my needs met. The bucket at the well is out of reach for me. I am *less than everyone else*; this leads us to experience life as victims.

EMBARRASSMENT   FAILURE   SUICIDAL

In the hospital at twenty-two months the most damaging consequence I picked up was the sense of shame. With the child's logic I knew I was unlovable. It was because of this my parents abandoned me and left me in pain because if I were loveable they would never have left me. For the next fifty years I carried a sense of shameful inferiority every day of my life and everywhere I went. You can see why it is often said to be toxic.

If I were to rob a bank it would be quite right for me to feel guilt and remorse as I would have done wrong. However, many of us feel a false guilt when there is no just cause, for it arises out of our twisted perception that 'we are less than anyone else', so we always fall short in our eyes whatever we do. Again the things we crave in our bucket are unreachable, whatever I do will never be good enough. Thus guilt and shame are common bedfellows.

GRIEF, LOSS AND SADNESS

Loss is as much part of the natural cycle of our lives as the seasons of the year and birth and death. We all will suffer loss in our lives. Loss is about losing someone or something that has supplied our needs both in a legitimate, godly way or as something from our bucket. It occurs inside and outside the Waterfall and can lead to a natural, godly grieving process though it may be complicated by our warped thinking and woundedness. A common complication is that we truncate the process and do not deal with the difficult aspects but bury them. This can lead to depression and a general blanket of sadness that can overlay a person's life.

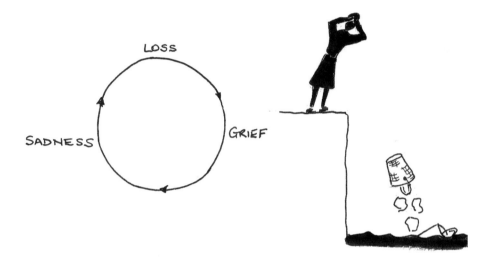

The pain we experience relates to the importance to us of the thing lost. The loss of a £20 note may only be minor to a lady 'doing lunch', a catastrophe to a Mum food shopping at the end of the month and a disaster to an addict wanting a 'fix'. It will trigger the same grieving process as the loss of a beloved parent or a long-held job. It is the intensity of the feelings and the depth of loss that is different as well as the meaning that loss has for us personally.

Grieving is a process that goes through different stages:

DENIAL and PROTEST – initially the loss is beyond our comprehension and we need facts and proof that it did indeed occur. We dispute the reality before us and only hard evidence will break through our defensive: "It can't have happened."

DESPAIR – a season of difficult feelings follows. Often there is anger and the need to blame someone, or guilt for things undone or unsaid. This is the darkest period and if the feelings are not dealt with it is possible to get stuck here for years and for depression to develop. Increasingly, the unfinished business of a lengthy litigation process can stop people moving on.

EXPLORATION – accepting the loss and facing the pain will allow the recovery phase to begin. This involves making the practical and emotional adjustments that are necessary to cope in the changed circumstances. There can be frequent lapses back into the despair phase which will lessen over time.

MOVING ON – letting go and moving on will look different for each person. Ideally, remembering with hope and finding meaning will eventually bring the courage to invest in new aspects of life.

The process is slow. Losing a life partner can take five years to work through. Often I meet people who are in this situation but a couple of months after the death they do not feel they can speak of their loss anymore because of other people's reactions or to protect others from pain. It was not understood in the past that children suffered loss and it was not acknowledged that they even needed a grieving process.

Loss of a job may lead to loss of competency, purpose and solvency. Injury may mean the loss of mobility, self image, dignity and independence. Loss is complicated and hits our very sense of identity. If you have suffered much loss in your life, talking with a bereavement counsellor can bring a lot of healing.

> **CAUTION: I am going to suggest in this section you do some exercises to help you to experience what we are describing. Please be sensitive to the Holy Spirit's leading and keep yourself safe. Your trusted spiritual companion will be invaluable if you need to talk and recording the journey will give you insights.**
>
> **I had ten years of counselling, two years of the Holy Spirit working alone with me on average doing a new thing every fortnight and God is still working in me but this is my walk, to prepare me for my healing ministry. God knows what you need and some of you reading this may need some form of help, to aid you as you explore your healing and equipping. If so, He will provide.**
>
> **However, I believe that to bring this to the wider church, to prepare so many of us for Jesus to return, only the Holy Spirit can get us ready. Only The Counsellor can do the scale of work needed to prepare us to be the army, ready for battle and to be the spotless bride of Christ. I believe God's heart in this is for us to learn to co-operate with the Holy Spirit in our healing and equipping. So let Him lead you.**

EXERCISE:
SPIDER DIAGRAM 1
To see the interaction of our inner world, choose a minor event on your timeline that stands out to you now. As you look at it, see if you can identify the feelings that it produced in you.
Below is an example using an event from my timeline.

- Go back to the event.
- Stick with it, try and get inside what was happening for you.
- Get in touch with what was going on inside you and feel the feelings again.

Let us just remind ourselves that we were born to have our deepest needs for love and belonging, for value and worth, and for meaning and purpose met in relationship with the Father.

When I am working with an individual, a helpful starting place is to expose and identify the feelings they have experienced. This tells us about how they perceive they are making progress towards their bucket and having their needs fulfilled.

If **ANGRY** they are feeling blocked from their goal of getting to their bucket and having their needs met.

If **ASHAMED** or **GUILTY** they do not feel they have the right to have their needs met and so the bucket is unreachable for them.

If **FEARFUL** they do not know whether they will reach the bucket or not and the uncertainty is crippling them.

HOPELESSNESS together with any of the negative feelings can cause **DEPRESSION**

Now let us turn our attention to what is going on in our thinking, which is the engine room that drives the choices we make and our subsequent behaviour.

REFLECTION
WHAT DO YOU BELIEVE
ABOUT YOURSELF?

Try asking a congregation, in any denomination, in any church, in any land how they are actually feeling right now and you will hear statements such as :-

I am lonely.
I have never belonged.
I'm on the outside.
No-one would love me.
I'm a waste of space.
I must be perfect.
They are all ok but I'm not. I'm not good enough.
I'm hopeless. I can't do it.
If they knew what I was really like......
I am less than everyone else. Why bother? I'm not loveable. I must be in control.

Capture what is going on inside for you.
What do you really believe about yourself?

OUR BELIEFS

We have seen that even as small babies we are picking up beliefs about ourselves and thereafter, we are adding evidence to confirm the rightness of what we believe. However, our observations as little people are neither accurate nor objective and yet they become the lenses through which we view the world as we grow up. It is like putting on a pair of tinted glasses with our beliefs colouring the lenses. If I believe

"I am a waste of space", every experience is coloured by that belief and that skews how I inhabit an experience and what I take from it.

Albert Ellis captured this in his ABC Theory of Perception. He said the way we feel about an event depends on what we believe about it. He labelled the stages of our inner journey:

A stands for an 'activating event' - something happens.

B stands for our 'belief' about the event.

C stands for the 'consequent emotion' we feel.

Lets see how this works:

When I was seven I caught scarlet fever. This was a serious condition in those far off days. I can vividly remember screaming and can still see the blue cow under the bed that was coming to get me. In the middle of the night I was collected by an ambulance, the doors closed on my parents and I was whisked off alone to an isolation hospital forty miles away from home. That proved again if you are in pain big people send you away, alone to a cot in the dark.

How bad could I be?

But it got worse. We did not have a car and at the weekend my parents had an arduous journey to come and visit me. In the ward the sick children could stand next to a glass window and parents could stand the other side, without contact. As soon as I saw my Mum and Dad I threw myself crying at the glass and I was so upset that the nurses waved my parents away. They had to turn and go back down the path. I did not see them again for another week, when the same thing happened again.

I was in hospital for three weeks. The day I was to be discharged I was taken from the isolation ward and put in a room on my own to await collection. I was in there, on my own, dressed and ready to go by 8am and still there at 8pm. The letter informing my parents of my discharge had been delivered to the wrong address. When eventually they arrived I would not speak to them and in my anger it was several weeks before I was 'normal'. The lessons of the two year old had been reinforced.

These lessons were the basis for critical life decisions as I grew up. I married a man who told me that if the 'love of his life' with whom he had broken up returned to him, he would leave me. I still married him because some love was better than no love, for someone who was unlovable and did not deserve to be loved for themselves.

He, too, was damaged and a victim. Professionally, he was an interrogator and knew how to break the SAS in their training. He could find my weakness. He would push my arm up behind my back and tell me to stop him by admitting my pain. I could not do that. It was only when I understood my story years later that I realised my response was fuelled by the belief that if you show pain you are abandoned. That belief robbed me of the power to stop the physical abuse. I allowed myself to be invaded.

These experiences came on the back of beliefs I already held about myself.

In the isolation hospital:

I held the belief (B) that I was unlovable. This was confirmed by the fact that (A) my parents let themselves be turned away from me, and finally did not even turn up to collect me, which left me angry (C). I would not speak to them. I was in effect saying, "I will make you hurt. I will give you nothing. I am punishing you for abandoning me again."

In my marriage:

I held the belief (B) that I was unlovable. That led me to marry a man who loved someone else (A) because I thought I could never be loved for myself. I felt shame (C). I felt that I had stolen a marriage and I did not want to be found out. This proved again how unworthy I was to be loved and confirmed again that I was 'less than' everyone else.

I held the belief (B) that I was unlovable, so I endured the physical abuse (A) because I could not admit that I was in pain. I was fearful (C) because I could not stand to be abandoned again.

....

In the fallen world, our thinking twists the shape of who we, are as we believe the lies we pick up along the way. When we have the awareness to work out what we believe, we can rectify the things we believe about ourselves. We need to listen to what God says about us. I believed that I was unlovable. That was a lie. God loves me. He always has!

So we Christians add two more letters to the ABC Theory:

D stands for 'Dispute the lie' - speaking against the ungodly things we have believed about ourselves

E stands for 'Exchange with the truth' - we are who God says we are, not who the world tells us we are. We need to replace the lies with God's truth.

Do not conform to the pattern of this world, but be transformed by the renewing of your mind. Then you will be able to test and approve what God's will is – his good, pleasing and perfect will. Romans 12:2

We are going to look at ways to rectify our ungodly thinking later in this chapter but there are one or two other points to note first.

NOTES

_____

_____

_____

_____

_____

_____

_____

_____

THE INNER VOICE

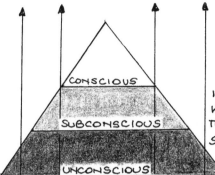

CONSCIOUS
IN OUR IMMEDIATE WORLD

SUBCONSCIOUS
IN OUR BRAIN'S FILING SYSTEM
WHICH CAN BE RETRIEVED BY
TRIGGERS SUCH AS SMELLS AND
SOUNDS OR BY CHOICE

UNCONSCIOUS
UNKNOWN DEPTHS HIDDEN
BY DEFENCE SYSTEMS OUR
STRATEGIES TO SURVIVE

THE DRIVERS FOR OUR
BEHAVIOUR COME FROM
OUR UNCONSCIOUS

As we understand our stories, we become aware of an inner voice feeding us the lies that have been lying buried in our unconscious. I became aware of a voice saying continuously, "I want to be loved. I'm not loveable. I want to be loved. I'm not loveable." Once you have tuned in, you can hear these tapes running through your mind, influencing every minute of your life. Even when you are not aware of them, these beliefs lying in your unconscious drive your behaviour.

When I walked into a room of new people, "I am not loveable" filled my head. Just think of the effect, everything about me would be sending out messages saying, "I am less than all of you and I do not expect you to want to know me."

An Iranian professor called Albert Mehrabian studied the three elements of face to face communications and he concluded that when concerned with feelings and attitudes (i.e. do we like this person) we understand each other 7% by words we use, 35% by the tone of voice we employ and 58% through our body language.

These figures are especially accurate when incongruence is present. So, for me I would not need to speak to signal the way I felt about myself to the whole room. There was a mismatch between trying to appear friendly and open on the outside and the truth inside. Moreover, this would be read by others and cause wariness, which in turn I would pick up, which confirmed to me that they did not want to know me because I was unlovable.

Reinforced by the vow I had made in the cot to abandon the world, I would hover on the edge of such gatherings, feeling isolated. I would be embarrassed if anyone spoke to me and run for cover as soon as I could. Thus what you believe leads you to behaviours that make them self-fulfilling prophecies and because in this scenario I would not be making a meaningful connection with anyone, again I would have the proof that I was unlovable. Also because I would believe that everyone else was okay I would be plunged deeper into a pit of shame and worthlessness.

EXERCISE:
SPIDER DIAGRAM 2

Taking what you did in the first exercise now add to it the things that you believed about yourself arising out of the event or reinforced by it. It helps to write down statements that are subjective.
For example:-

I'm unlovable.   I must keep the peace.
I'm responsible.   I can't do it.
I'll never be any good.   I always get it wrong.

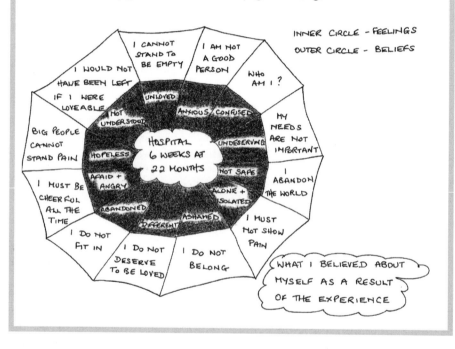

RIGHT AND WRONG

In the Fall the disobedience, which led to the eating of the fruit from the Tree of the Knowledge of Good and Evil, corkscrewed our thinking away from alignment with God's will and purposes. The characteristic of fallen thinking is that we **THINK** we know right from wrong, we **THINK** we know what is best for our families, for our churches and for our own life. I always tried to do my best but I played God trying to survive and to make life work. I was not very good at it. Looking back, I caused so much damage and unhappiness. I became what most victims become and that is an agent of harm. Playing God was exhausting, I was so relieved when I could give it up and stand in the Waterfall and let God be God.

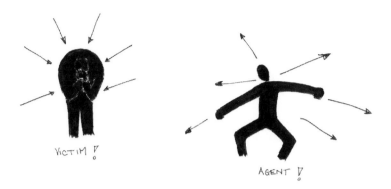

VICTIM V

AGENT V

WHAT YOU BELIEVE MATTERS

There was a coherence in all the Trinity did. Now when we walk in the footsteps of Jesus in the Waterfall we can become effective tools as we come into alignment with God's heart and mind. But where are we now? Our mind is the engine room of the whole of our functioning, what state is it in? The truth is as we enter the Waterfall our minds need to be rebuilt and thereafter require regular servicing. Bill Johnson puts it this way:-

> **"All attitudes, beliefs, expectations, decisions, agreements, vows and oaths that do not agree with God's WORD, NATURE or CHARACTER are ungodly."**

If we are believing what the world believes, we are doing Satan's work for him! Mark Virkler has researched how much of our thinking as Christians is negative.

NEGATIVE THOUGHT PATTERNS

"The accuser accuses; the Comforter comforts," says Mark Virkler. He argues that every negative thought is from the enemy and every positive, life-giving, upbuilding thought is always of the Holy Spirit. Just as the Lord speaks to us in a still small voice saying, *"This is the way, walk in it." (Isaiah 30:21)* so Satan does the same. Which is which? The answer lies in the content.

Mark Virkler's research led him to believe that on average as born-again Christians 80% of our thought life is negative. He says we are critical, accusatory, judgemental, and smug. Our speech is about problems and injustices; we fixate on what people have done or not done, for us or to us. We hold onto our hurts and attempt to find justification for our actions. We spend much time comparing ourselves unfavourably to others and envying them.

The enemy loves this.

The renewing of our mind is accomplished by exchanging the lies we have believed with the truth and replacing worldly thinking with God's wisdom. So as we journey God will be showing us where our thinking is skewed and where His truth is to be found. Deepening our relationship with God and getting to know His Word will help us enter into His world.

We can see that in our pain we often enter into ungodly thinking because of our experience and circumstances. Words may be spoken over us that become a curse upon our lives, "You will never amount to anything." A throwaway, thoughtless word at the wrong time can become the precept by which we live our lives. A vow comes with chains that may cripple us in growth and rob us of happiness.

I said earlier that I made a vow when I was in the hospital at twenty-two months of age. I was waiting for a doctor to come in to the room to see me. I was getting better and was no longer strapped down so the doctor would pick me up and hold me. It was the only kind connection there was in that place. When at last he came he would not pick me up as I was wet and needed changing. He turned round and walked out. The nurse who changed me was angry with me for getting her into trouble and her hands, voice and tone delivered a damning message to me.

At this point I had had it with grown ups. Abandoned by Mum and Dad who could not stand pain, rejected by my nice doctor and unjustly blamed and reviled by the nasty nurse, I made the decision to abandon the world. It was just too painful a place to be and rather than wait for the next kick in the teeth, I got in first. I erected a glass wall between the world and myself.

It was fifty years before I renounced that vow. Actually, I had no idea I had made a vow until I had counselling and the Holy Spirit brought it to the surface. However, the effects of it were visible throughout my story.

NOTES

_____

_____

_____

_____

_____

_____

_____

_____

_____

_____

_____

_____

_____

_____

_____

_____

_____

HOW DO I DO THAT?
CHANGING MY THINKING

There is a simple step by step process which will help you to play your part in changing your thinking, when it is the right time.
This will result in the 'renewing of your mind' and your coming to maturity.

1. RECOGNISE the lie or the ungodly thought. Be self-aware. You will become more adept at 'hearing' what you think as you journey onwards. Stop sometimes and try and capture what is going on in your inner world, listen to your inner voice.

2. REPENT and say sorry for living out of the lie. Receiving forgiveness gives you freedom and a clean slate to reframe what you believe.

3. RENOUNCE the lie or vow, break its power. " I renounce this expectation of me.....(Speak it out) or I break this vow to.....(and name it) IN THE NAME OF JESUS."

4. REPLACE the lie with the Truth. What does God say? The Bible is your richest resource. Find a specific Scripture to digest that refutes the old belief. The Father's Love Letter is a great place to start. *(see Appendix)*

5. RECEIVE the truth. The lies you have believed are part of the way you have habitually viewed yourself and the world. You have to break the habit. Each time the thought is in your head dispute the lie. I hold my hand up and say aloud, **"Stop. That is a lie. I do not accept it."** Then repeat the truth. Actively repeat the truth through the day. Write it down. Savour it and most importantly act out of the new truth. David said the Word was a *"lamp to his feet and honey to his lips",* his guide and sustenance.

6. RELEASE blessings. Ask God to specifically release blessings into the area that was previously difficult, so that it not only is no longer a problem but becomes a strength.

When I understood my vow to 'abandon the world' I could see the harmful effects that it had caused throughout my story. I needed to repent of the thought and for the consequences. I renounced the vow but it was then the real work of renewal began for me.

The vow had caused there to be a glass wall between me and the world, further confirming that I was unlovable and for me to feel I was 'less than' everyone else. I felt disconnected and apart from others, making my world a very lonely place. In counselling I described it as being adrift in far, dark space. Replacing the lies implicit in all this and receiving the truth took some time.

The glass wall down, my defences gone, I needed to move out towards others. It felt very risky. In this place of vulnerability I began by telling myself that I was loved by my Father in heaven. I said it continually. I was helped by hearing Selwyn Hughes, his arms open wide, say that love is walking towards others without self-protection. He said it was what Jesus did on the Cross and that image kept giving me the courage to keep going forward, towards people. You will find the Holy Spirit will give you encouragement and the particular thing that will help you.

I had to learn to how to relate on a deep level and change the way I valued myself. This took time because it was living life out of a completely new place for me. I also had to be active in disputing the lies. It did not matter if I did not feel loveable. I had to accept the truth that I am. I chose Scriptures to confirm this and decided to believe them.

....

This is all about learning to live in the Waterfall, where I am who God says I am. The truth is that I am not 'less than' anyone else but I am the daughter of my Father, the High King of heaven.

When this truth that you are of God's family, the son or daughter of the King, a member of the royal priesthood, created for God's purpose, sinks into your being, this new perspective changes the way you experience life.

There is a power when we know who we are. Jesus amazed the listeners in Matthew 8 because He spoke out of His authority which flowed from His knowing who He was. I believe Ephesians is the book of the Waterfall and for us to be all we were created to be, we need to embrace the truths written there.

CHOICES

Often when we are wounded it seems as though we are robbed of the ability to make choices in our life. It is as though we are pre-programmed to follow a certain line, the drivers for which are seated in our unconscious. Part of our healing is to become aware that we are choosing beings and can make healthy choices. One of the gifts God gave us was free will but few of us are fit enough to exercise it.

Living in the Waterfall we stand on a firm foundation; our pressing need for love and belonging, value and worth, meaning and purpose being met through our relationship with the Father. Outside the Waterfall, instead of life on the rock, we are balancing on a pin surviving, getting what we can where we can. Though we may not be aware of it along the way we are making two sorts of choices.

Firstly, we do things to try and protect ourselves, to survive. These are our defence mechanisms. We build a cage of behaviours around us to make ourselves feel safe. We can hide away behind shyness, humour, aggression, bullying, denial, spiritualising, fantasy, rationalising, hypochondria, control and withdrawal. The list of mechanisms is endless as we are very creative about the way we protect ourselves. They give us the illusion we are safe and that no-one will find out the big secret that we are only acting out being okay.

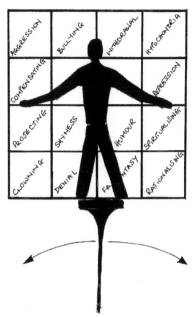

BUILDING THE ILLUSION OF BEING SAFE!

Secondly, we have seen that when outside the Waterfall at our very core we all have emptiness. The second set of choices we make is designed to try and fill the void and to try make us feel good, masking that emptiness inside. So we often drive to be the best in some area; the perfect parent, the perfect Christian or the most spiritual, the one who never says 'no', or we go for status, or for being the top of the pile. If the world thinks we are great it must be so. Then we may use all sorts of ways to fill the ache inside: chocolate, sex, drugs, shopping, alcohol, the newest gadgets, celebrity and fame.

FILLING THE EMPTINESS INSIDE GIVES
US THE ILLUSION WE ARE OK!

EXERCISE:
SPIDER DIAGRAM 3

What choices did you make arising out of the event you are exploring. What behaviours resulted from it?

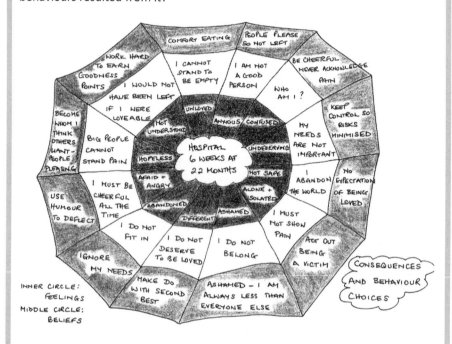

Add the third layer to your diagram.

IDENTITY

At the core of who we are is our sense of identity. We draw our sense of this from our belief system which flows out of our choices and experience. Outside the Waterfall our identity is based on what we think the world says about us.

At one stage in my life I had to be the 'best trainer in the world'. My second marriage was at a disastrous stage where we were both damaging each other daily. Work was the best place to be and in the commercial liability insurance claims department of a global insurance company a position was created for me which involved training staff and management. I had arrived! I was someone! I was good at what I did and prided myself on glitzy presentations

that delivered. They took a great deal of energy and if someone said, "Well done!" at the end of it, I got a little bit of what I needed in my bucket, some approval, some worth, some meaning. However, as I drove home it leaked out. Home filled me with loneliness, hopelessness and anger and such a sense of failure and self-loathing that going into work the following morning I would be anxious. Would I be found out for who I really was?

I would have to try harder to get the same reaction I had achieved the day before. Each day I was working harder and harder, more and more desperate to get something in my bucket from the participants. If no-one praised me I immediately went into the 'I am a worthless failure' mode on the inside, whilst showing a smiling 'I'm in control' exterior to the outside world.

What was happening here? My sense of identity depended wholly on what I thought people thought about me. If they were approving I got something in my bucket but it did not last and the next time I had to try harder to make the same impression. Without being aware of it my whole focus was on getting my needs met. I did not have the capacity to be aware of others because of the overwhelming nature of the thirsts driving me. I was so busy manipulating others to try and provide for my needs I had no energy left for caring for them. However, I could not let them know that, so I played the game of being concerned.

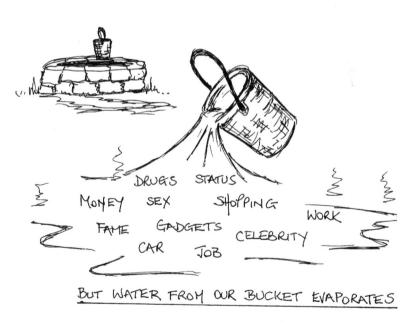

BUT WATER FROM OUR BUCKET EVAPORATES

I need to state again I was completely unaware of these contradictions in my inner story. At that time I sincerely believed that I was spending my life working for the good of others.

As my inner story was so at odds with the outside I was acting out, inside I became emptier and emptier. The exhaustion of trying to fill the void kept building until it led to my implosion and breakdown when Jesus saved me. This shows how the things we rely on to supply our needs cannot sustain us. Only filled, in the Waterfall of God's love, with our identity in who God says we are, is it possible to live authentic lives where there is no contradiction between our inner and outer worlds.

UNDERSTANDING OUR STORY AND MAKING CHANGES

When we understand our past story we can begin to make decisions about how we want to live in the future. When I drew out my story I could see immediately how I had tried to play God in my life and that there was an alternate way of living, God's way. It came as an enormous relief as I was exhausted from trying to make life work.

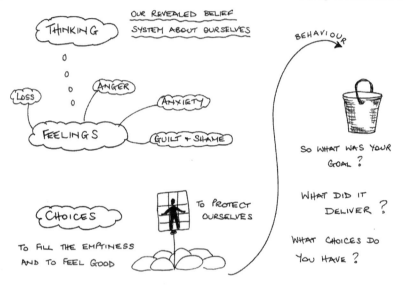

Perhaps using the above diagram draw the threads of your story together, reflecting on your timeline and spider diagrams.

NOTES

START WITH YOUR FEELINGS

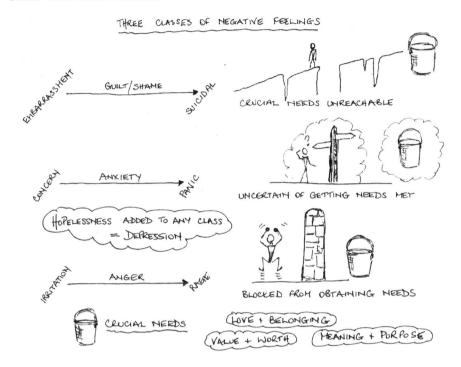

Write down all the feelings you have discovered in yourself. Attach them to the class of feeling that is most appropriate. You probably have some feelings attached to each class but tune in and see which is causing you the most trouble in this aspect of your story. This diagram will remind you of what we have learnt about feelings. What is the most painful feeling for you? This will tell you something about how you perceive your progress towards your goal and your bucket.

YOUR GOAL will be where, how or with what you believe you can get your needs met for love and belonging, value and worth and meaning and purpose. Can you identify the goal you have been chasing?

NOW YOUR THINKING - WHAT DO YOU BELIEVE ABOUT YOURSELF?
List the statements
e.g. I must keep everyone happy.
I'm not good enough

THEN YOUR CHOICES - What behaviours and actions do you use to get your needs met at your bucket down your well? There are two sorts of choices we make:-

CHOICE A)   What have you done to try and keep safe?
e.g. I have withdrawn from others so I do not get hurt.
I control people and my surroundings.

CHOICE B) What have you done to feel good about yourself and to fill the emptiness inside?

e.g. I seek the approval of others - if they say I am okay I must be okay.
I binge on chocolate.
I must win at all costs.

What do your choices tell you about where and what you have been relying on to deliver your needs for

LOVE and BELONGING
VALUE and WORTH
MEANING and PURPOSE?

WHAT WERE YOUR GOALS?

Let us remember we were created to have these crucial needs met firstly through our relationship with the FATHER. If we have looked elsewhere we have been creating idols and have sinned.

However, now we understand our story we can consider how to change the situation.

WHAT DO I WANT MY NEW GODLY GOALS TO BE?

NOTES

_____
_____
_____
_____
_____
_____
_____
_____
_____
_____
_____
_____
_____
_____
_____
_____
_____
_____

ACTIVITY
Pull together the threads of your inner story and reflect on what it tells you.

THE BEGINNING OF CHANGE starts with understanding our story:

- *seeing and understanding God's intention for us*
- *realising why we have been going to the cistern*
- *recognising the beliefs that drove us there*
- *recognising the consequences in our lives*

STEPS TO CHANGE

There are three areas to work on:

1. By making a decision to live in the Waterfall, the place God intended for us to dwell, we enter a new phase of our relationship with Him. We can choose to believe what God says about us, to draw our identity and needs from Him, embracing Kingdom living with all its practical implications for our lives.
2. We can consciously choose new goals for our life in line with Godly principles. Selwyn Hughes used to suggest that our goal should be 'to live a life that is pleasing to God'. We then can break this down into the specific areas which God reveals to us as we follow His leading.
3. We need to actively work on rectifying our thinking to bring it into line with the Truth.

These three areas take time, work and attention to become the new reality of our lives. The outworking of these areas are the framework for our ongoing journey in the Waterfall.

The journey is encapsulated in the whole book of Ephesians :

> *You were taught with regard to your former way of life, to put off your old self, which is being corrupted by its deceitful desires; to be made new in the attitude of your minds; and to put on the new self, created to be like God in true righteousness and holiness. Ephesians 4: 22-24*

Having understood our story, now let us try and pull together what we have learned

All of us have our own stories, our own pain; we are complex beings, many strands make up the tapestry of who we are. However, the Holy Spirit is the Counsellor. Healing is a big part of the journey of the disciple. God wants to straighten out the distortions in our image so that we are clear channels for His power; He wants to set us free from our wounds and the burden of the lies we have believed; and He wants to use that experience to comfort others and to spread the light of His truth. Standing in the Waterfall and believing this allows us to co-operate in the process. However, it is not for us to go digging in our past. The Holy Spirit will signal the next thing on His agenda for us by bringing it to our attention, often by an emotional over-reaction that erupts from a situation.

The first important question is "Are you willing to let Him heal you?" This is not agreed to without thought – all healing involves pain. The good news is what the Holy Spirit starts, He finishes. Saying "Yes" is saying yes to receiving that which Jesus died to give you: freedom and wholeness.

 THE PROMISE OF JESUS
You are safe, the Holy Spirit will lead you individually. Jesus promises:

A bruised reed he will not break, and a smouldering wick he will not snuff out. Matthew 12:20

When you have spent a lifetime avoiding pain it takes courage to go there, especially if at this moment your faith is not quite strong enough for you to believe that God is going to do these things FOR YOU. That is okay I believe for you. I make extravagant promises for God based not on what He has done for me, not what I have seen Him do for others but because He is, who He says He is. God cannot act outside His character and the fact is if you are committing your life to Him in the Waterfall Romans 8 :28 comes into play, so I can stand on His Word for you.

And we know that in all things God works for the good of those who love him, who have been called according to his purpose.

So much of life in the Waterfall is getting hold of this robust view, that God is good and great and powerful and faithful and His face is turned towards YOU. He needs us to respond to Him and take all He has given us in Jesus Christ and by the Holy Spirit because He has chosen to use us in His story. Come on the healing journey and then you can play your full part in the Kingdom.

Do not fear for I have redeemed you; I have summoned you by name; you are mine. When you pass through the rivers, they will not sweep over you. When you walk through the fire, you will not be burned; the flames will not set you ablaze. Isaiah 42:12

HOW DO I DO THAT?
UNDERSTANDING THE HEALING PROCESS

1. SOMETHING ERUPTS

When you become aware of a discordant emotion or a feeling that is unexpectedly strong, the question to ask the Holy Spirit is, "What is going on here?" Understand a healing lesson is starting. We know that the Holy Spirit could and does occasionally heal instantly but the process of healing is also part of preparing us for our ministry. With the comfort we receive we will comfort others so there are many things He needs us to learn as we go through the process.

2. COLLECT THE CLUES

Once the Holy Spirit has highlighted the beginning of a phase of healing, He will be bringing things that are relevant to light. Often memories, long-forgotten, will pop into your mind. He will orchestrate circumstances and experiences that He will speak through to help your understanding.
Reflect and look for clues, be aware and be expectant. Record them.

3 CO-OPERATE

Do the things that are suggested in this chapter: the timeline, investigating your feelings, exploring the underlying beliefs you hold about yourself, looking at your choices. Use the spider diagrams and your journal. If you need the help of another person the Holy Spirit will provide them for you. Often it is helpful just to talk things through with another person, but sometimes we need more expertise from the listener. Go with what you feel in your head and your heart when considering this.

4. DRAW OUT YOUR STORY

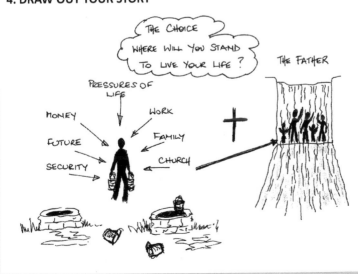

5. CHOOSE
Reflect on where you have been acting independently from the Father. If you want to change things choose a new course of action.

6. REPENT
Ask forgiveness of the Father and turn away from your cistern through the Cross of Jesus and into the Waterfall of the Father's presence.

7. FORGIVE
Forgive anyone who has injured you. Do not forget to forgive yourself. (There is a section on Forgiveness further on in the book.)

8. WATERFALL PERSPECTIVES
Choose a Godly goal to replace what you sought in your bucket, e.g. if you were striving to become the perfect Christian and what people thought of you had fed you in the past, you could choose to be a good Christian:
- *Doing the things God wants you to do and not saying yes to everything.*
- *Making choices in line with God's will and purpose for you.*
- *Doing things that would please God.*

This takes time and thought and exploration to adjust your life and to get used to living out of the new place.
- *Dispute the lies you have believed and replace them with the truth.*
- *Actively, seek your identity in what God says about you.*

The Bible is a rich resource to reframe these two areas.

9. LETTING GO OF PAIN
When all is understood and the threshold of freedom is a step away, some people experience their most difficult battle. It can seem so huge to let go of the pain and grasp the hope set before you. When you discover how pain has ruled your life it suddenly seems like a friend. If it is all you have known, you may question what will life be like in the future without it: the unknown is a dangerous place. Some people feel if they give it up who will they then be? Does the pain you have suffered give you your identity? Ultimately, it is a choice to let go and move on, that means a decision not a feeling. Actually, feelings will never change ahead of your thinking so we need to be prepared to take the risk.

The more you trust in the character of the Father, the less risky it becomes. Often a simple physical act can help the process of release by burning a paper, stepping over the line, changing your name. This was done by a lady who came on a course. She had a revelation that as Sue she had never been valued or listened to and as she understood her story she decided henceforth she wanted to be known as Susan.

As you see things flowing out of you, picture the Waterfall thundering down, drenching you inside and out and washing away the hurts and cleansing your wounds. Filling you with the crystal water of the River of Life that flows from the Throne of Heaven, bringing life where it flows.

It may take a long time to be free. If you are struggling, do seek someone to walk beside you. I hold hope for people who are dealing with dark feelings of the past for this is the ministry of the Holy Spirit and the landscape of our journey does change.

10. SEE THE PATTERN

Though I had many years of counselling from a professional, I also had a sustained two year period of counselling from the Holy Spirit.

Typically, we went through a lesson every couple of weeks. I would go through the above stages so that I would understand the bit of my story that was under the spotlight and then there would be some challenge attached to my healing, from the Holy Spirit and a narrow gate with Jesus the other side. I remember one occasion when I was carrying a backpack and it would not fit through the narrow gate, only I could get through. The challenge usually led to me having a forty-eight hour tantrum while Jesus waited patiently. It usually took me that long to run out of steam and then consider and go through to the joy of Jesus' welcome and a new spiritual landscape. Part of the importance of sharing this process is, I believe, that the Holy Spirit wants to do business directly with each disciple and knowing how to co-operate will facilitate this.

Choices

JESUS chose the road to JERUSALEM

Deut. 30:19
This day I call heaven and earth as witnesses against you that I have set before you life and death, blessings and curses. Now choose life, so that you and your children may live.

Exodus 32:26
So he stood at the entrance to the camp and said, "Whoever is for the Lord, come to me." And all the Levites rallied to him.

Ruth 1:16
But Ruth replied, 'Don't urge me to leave you or to turn back from you. Where you go I will go; and where you stay I will stay. Your people will be my people and your God, my God.

CHOSEN BY GOD 1 PETER 2:9
But you are a chosen people, a royal priesthood, a holy nation, a people belonging to God, that you may declare the praises of him who called you out of darkness into his wonderful light.

I could ask my Father for thousands of angels and he would send them instantly. But if I did, how would the Scriptures be fulfilled that describe what is happening now?

Psalm 119:30
I have chosen the way of truth; I have set my heart on your laws.

Joshua 24:15
But if serving the Lord seems undesirable to you, then choose for yourselves this day whom you will serve, whether the gods your forefathers served beyond the river or the gods of the Amorites, in whose land you are living. But as for me and my household we will serve the Lord.

 *As you know by now, I had had much counselling and had understood much of the impact and experience I had endured at twenty-two months, having fractured my skull and been in hospital for six weeks. However, whilst tutoring, something triggered an unexpected anger in me. It was a surprise because at that time I did not 'do' anger; it was still too frightening and buried deep. I knew this was the start of another healing lesson from the Holy Spirit.*

What was revealed in the next two weeks was all my anger against the doctors and the system and the impact of the injury on my life. The major image for me was of the little person raging against being strapped down in the cot and the feel of the straps around my wrists. My anger crystallised into a fury against Jesus for not being there.

Having understood the impact, it was the time for the healing of this memory. I went back to that time in the hospital room in my mind and I saw Jesus there. I poured out to Him all my anger, not holding anything back, a small child raging out her despair and blackness. Jesus picked me up and I suddenly realised He had been there all the time and KNEW that I had never been alone or abandoned. I was able then to forgive the doctors and the nurses and was ready to move on.

However, that was not the finish: the Holy Spirit then asked me to have my wrists tied to go through the narrow gate. Writing this now I can feel again my volcanic reactions, the stomach churning, the panic of being tied, the wanting to throw myself about. I had my two day tantrum.

Jesus was waiting patiently beyond the narrow gate. The Holy Spirit held the rope and I was exhausted. Feelings expended, I could now think and make my choice. Would I let the Holy Spirit tie my wrists? Did I trust Jesus? What else would I do ? Where else would I go? So I let the Holy Spirit bind my wrists and I went through. Jesus did not release me immediately but He showed me that I was deeper in and higher up, than I had ever been and there were things ahead worth any cost. One morning soon after Jesus came and untied my wrists.

On that day I was in the process of buying a new yellow Skoda which I had already dubbed my sunshine car. The purchase of it was something of a financial miracle, which was God's provision and so I was feeling very blessed. The garage rang with the number so I could arrange the insurance. It was 298 COT. I heard God chuckle! So the bleakness of the images in the hospital that had recently been so vivid were released and replaced by what was then universally known as 'The Sunshine Cot'. A gift from God on so many levels.

TAKING JESUS THERE

It is the work of the Holy Spirit to help us to understand our stories and to implement change but it is Jesus who will minister, in very personal and creative ways, our healing and wholeness.

Therefore, to involve Jesus in our inner story as well as our outward walk is another aspect of discipleship to learn. There are many occasions when taking Jesus there to our inner world brings enlightenment, comfort or healing.

Enlightenment

At a retreat recently God gave us a prophecy. The following is part of it.

> *"I have gathered and led you to the mountain top. Standing here you can see what I see. Now the veil will fall away. If you are unsure meet me here and we will look together. Meet me in your spirit here on the mountain top and I will share what I see."*

If I shut my eyes and imagine myself on the summit I can stand beside Jesus and ask Him to show me what I need to know. He will respond to my questions and concerns so that I may fulfil my part in His story.

We have a bigger part to play than we can imagine. In the flow of the Spirit in the Waterfall we are aligned to the will and purposes of God, who then trusts us to join Him in His work. The closer we stay to Jesus and the more we seek His view the bigger the part we can play.

> *I am the Lord ... who carries out the words of his servants and fulfils the predictions of His messengers. Isaiah 44: 26*

Comfort

It is open to us all to have a special, safe and personal place we can go in our spirit to meet with Jesus and spend time with Him. It might be a beach, beside a waterfall, a bedroom. If the world has never been a safe place for you this can be especially precious. Choose in your imagination a location that is meaningful, warm and secure and meet Jesus there. There as you converse you will get to know Him well and build a relationship that has depth and significance.

Healing

When the Holy Spirit has been at work in us to restore our broken image and we begin to replace the lies we have believed with God's truth, the damage that underpins the distortions will be raw. There are likely to be hidden wounds, uncomfortable memories and unanswerable questions that need the touch of Jesus.

NOTES

_____

_____

_____

_____

_____

_____

_____

_____

HOW DO I DO THAT?
TAKE JESUS THERE

1. In your imagination go back to the event, the time and place that concerns you. Be back there, be aware of what surrounded you, the sights and sounds and smells - feel how you felt.

2. Now stand outside the picture - observing yourself in the scene - Jesus is beside you. Pour out your heart to Him. Don't hold back but allow yourself to be brutally honest about the way you think and feel.

3. AND Jesus will respond. Listen to what He wants to say to you. Jesus will always act within His character and He will speak to you.

4. Healing is a process and sometimes we need to learn more before a resolution. Involving Jesus at an early stage in your healing journey allows Him to give you the love, comfort, revelation and the strength you need for the next part of your walk.

5. Often after the talking is done, Jesus will spontaneously take action. When I poured out the pain of my heart about my experience as the baby in hospital. Jesus walked over to the cot and picked me up. At once my life's perspective changed. I KNEW Jesus had been there all the time. I WAS NEVER ALONE. I felt his love and my life view transformed.

6. When healing people Jesus often asked, 'What do you want?' You can ask Jesus for what you want Him to do for you. Let Him remove the burdens you hold inside you, unlock the chains, touch the wounds, mend your broken heart. Jesus is willing. It is why He came:

   The Spirit of the Sovereign Lord is on me, because the Lord has anointed me to preach good news to the poor.
   He has sent me to bind up the brokenhearted, to proclaim freedom for the captives and release from darkness for the prisoners, to proclaim the year of the Lord's favour and the day of vengeance of our God, to comfort all who mourn, and provide for those who grieve in Zion - to bestow on them a crown of beauty instead of ashes, the oil of gladness instead of mourning and a garment of praise instead of a spirit of despair. Isaiah 61:1-3

7. Do you need to forgive? Do you need to forgive yourself?

8. Thank Jesus for what He has done.

9. Don't give up if what is in play is not yet completed. This means there is more that God needs you to know and learn. Keep asking the Holy Spirit to show you, involve Jesus and at the right time God's healing will come. He always finishes what He starts.

MINISTRY MATTERS

My ministry is about encouraging and growing disciples. It is about helping people to travel to wholeness and to mature spiritually. It is very much about transforming pain. We can only take people where we have been willing to go and so not only has it been a long journey but it is a present one. Pain has changed for me. I can well remember in the early days as soon as I understood my pain I would want to offload it as quickly as possible onto Jesus but one day He came and asked me to carry it. I understand now, that it is important that if you are working in any form of healing ministry, staying close to the pain you have experienced keeps you authentic. However, it was not the raw pain Jesus handed back but the pain He had transformed; now it brings me blessing because I minister out of it. Pain is never far away but now I'm on the inside, in the Waterfall and in trusting God I am privileged to work with God 'shoulder to shoulder', expecting and seeing His sovereign answers as the high adventure continues.

> Then I will purify the lips of the peoples, that all of them may call on the name of the Lord and serve Him shoulder to shoulder. Zephaniah 3: 9

In God's wide plan we all have unique ministries and all of us need some measure of healing on the way to wholeness but what is certain is that God wants us all in the Waterfall of His love. As we trust, He can open doors that bring others in. The tears you have shed will not be wasted but treasured in God's economy and will be part of your gifting that brings fruit for the Kingdom.

> Restore our fortunes, O Lord like streams in the Negev. Those who sow in tears will reap with songs of joy. He who goes out weeping will return with songs of joy, carrying sheaves with him. Psalm 126: 4 – 6

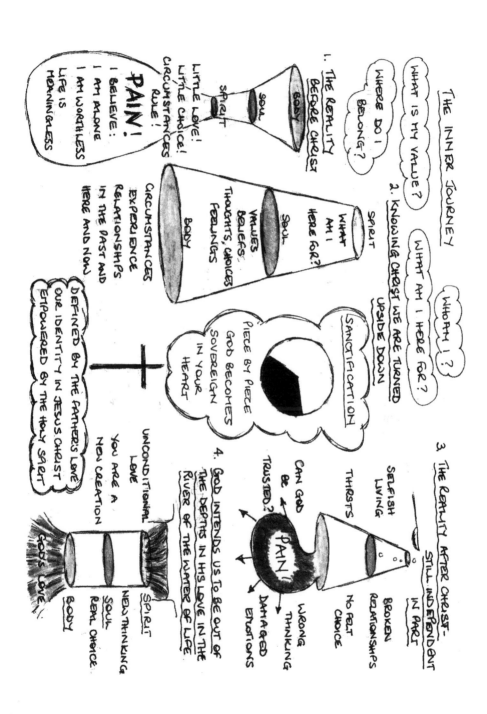

THE INNER JOURNEY

WHAT IS MY VALUE?

WHERE DO I BELONG?

1. THE REALITY BEFORE CHRIST

SPIRIT
SOUL
BODY

LITTLE LOVE!
LITTLE CHOICE!
CIRCUMSTANCES RULE!

PAIN!
I BELIEVE:
I AM ALONE
I AM WORTHLESS
LIFE IS MEANINGLESS

2. KNOWING CHRIST WE ARE TURNED UPSIDE DOWN

WHO AM I?

WHAT AM I HERE FOR?

SPIRIT
WHAT AM I HERE FOR?

SOUL
VALUES:
BELIEFS:
THOUGHTS, CHOICES
FEELINGS

BODY
CIRCUMSTANCES
EXPERIENCE
RELATIONSHIPS
IN THE PAST AND
HERE AND NOW

SANCTIFICATION

PIECE BY PIECE
GOD BECOMES
SOVEREIGN
IN YOUR
HEART

DEFINED BY THE FATHER'S LOVE
OUR IDENTITY IN JESUS CHRIST
EMPOWERED BY THE HOLY SPIRIT

3. THE REALITY AFTER CHRIST - STILL INDEPENDENT

IN PART

SELFISH LIVING

BROKEN RELATIONSHIPS

THIRSTS

NO FELT CHOICE

CAN GOD BE TRUSTED?

WRONG THINKING

PAIN!

DAMAGED EMOTIONS

4. GOD INTENDS US TO BE OUT OF THE DEPTHS IN HIS LOVE IN THE RIVER OF THE WATER OF LIFE

UNCONDITIONAL LOVE

YOU ARE A NEW CREATION

SPIRIT
NEW THINKING

SOUL
REAL CHOICE

BODY

GOD'S LOVE

PART THREE
CONVERSING WITH GOD, HEART TO HEART

INTRODUCTION

If the Waterfall is the place you choose to stand to live your life you will find you have joined God in a new reality that brings Him to life, up front and personal in every facet of your life. In the next three chapters we explore some of the ways we can have confidence that we can converse with Him and know His mind.

As from God before God in Christ we speak.
2 Corinthians 2:17

CHAPTER 6

HAVE YOU HEARD FROM GOD ?

Between any two people the vital spark that ignites a relationship is the way they make themselves known to each other. When we meet someone whom we sense may be important to us, we invest time in getting to know them. Actually we are making all sorts of judgements at every level of our being about the other person, to decide at what level we want to be involved with them. Attraction and trust are being assessed.

When we speak, the words we use convey only a small part of our meaning. There are many other subtle messages we pick up from each other, including body language and voice tone which help us understand what is being conveyed. However, it is a complex and many faceted process to grow into a deep relationship with another person. The bond is a living thing that needs continual attention to develop into an intimate and sustaining life force.

Life is about relationships, families are about relationships, God is about relationships. All our relationships are unique and are characterised by the different ways we choose to communicate with that person.

Often we block out what God would say to us because we cannot believe He would stoop to our low level and engage with us BUT that is not the evidence. God is inviting us into His family, into His story. He is sharing His heart with us and the things He values most. The message is clear: God wants to have a close, personal relationship with each one of us.

EVERYTHING BEGINS WITH GOD

I had a vicar say to me, "I would not want to say God actually spoke to me." It was a reprimand. I had said I'd heard directly from God and he was making it clear that God was so majestic and holy that it was arrogance and blasphemy on my part to claim to speak with Him. The inference was that God would not stoop so low.

Yesterday a preacher said that in Old Testament times God spoke directly to Samuel BUT in these days He speaks through His Word. Why are people so scared of recognising that our creative God can use all manner of ways to speak with His people now? Why do we want to limit Him so? We say in truth our God is the same yesterday, today, and forever, except He will not speak to us face to face any more. That just does not make sense when He has gone to so much trouble to have the living relationship with us restored. It is saying that since Jesus, God has closed down channels He used many times in the Old Testament for people such as Abraham, Samuel and David to become intimate with Him. Surely, after the death and resurrection of Jesus and the restoration of mankind through the forgiveness of sins, God is not going to limit Himself on how He speaks with us?

If we say God cannot now speak directly to His people, the cause of the unease may be a false humility. We do not want to appear arrogant. However, we have started in the wrong place by comparing ourselves to God and finding ourselves unworthy. So we shut down God. We forget that God invited us into His story, He is in control and He can do anything He pleases. The Father offered Jesus as sacrifice so we could be back in the Waterfall of His presence, talking with Him. He gave us the Holy Spirit to facilitate the flow of understanding between us. He has done it; the channels are open. He wants to speak to us, He needs to speak to us. How else can we grow in discipleship and friendship with our God, nurtured and sustained and moving in His will and purpose?

WHY GOD NEEDS TO SPEAK WITH US

Look at it from the Father's point of view: He created us to be in His family. Loving relationships need loving communication, texting is not always the answer!

He invites us to be involved in His story – He needs to tell us what part we are to play and when to act.

REFLECTION : Spend some time pondering these truths
God needs to train us so we know how we are to be involved in effective ways for the Kingdom.

- The Father sacrificed His Son. PLEASE HEAR THIS, IT COST HIM DEAR, HIS MOST PRECIOUS SON, so we can come again into His presence and be in the deep, intimate relationship He created us to have with Himself.
- It is a love story. He wants us to experience this.
- Jesus came to model how it works.
- The Father gave us the Holy Spirit and in the Waterfall we are connected heart to heart with the living God.

As we see God's eager anticipation for closeness with us, what is our response?

GOD IS WAITING FOR US TO BELIEVE

I tutor on a People Helpers' course. We share how the living God is naturally involved in the healing process because it is the Holy Spirit who is The Counsellor. Sometimes it is a cause of some scepticism or pain when we talk openly to participants of God speaking to us.

One lady said to me, "It's alright for you, God talks to you but He would never talk to me." Well I have learnt to make outrageous promises for God and that is not taking Him for granted but believing that God will always act within His character. So I suggested that she go outside into the grounds and sit under a tree. I told her to shut up and listen and that God would speak to her before tea which was 20 minutes away. She was back within five, beaming and shrieking, "He spoke to me, He spoke to me!" It was a very hot day and so before going outside she had gone to her room to get a hat and to apply some sunscreen. As she put the cream on her face God said to her, "That is what you do to me. You put a barrier between us."

Why did she hear then? God was always there. Perhaps it was because this time she expected to hear and as soon as she listened expectantly she heard God's voice speaking. If we expect God to speak it is like picking up the receiver knowing we are going to hear.

THE WOUNDED DEAF

I don't know how many times I have heard people say, "God does not speak to me!" The subtext of this statement can be various but, "He would not talk to me because I am not worthy" is common. What is that but the cry of loss and pain, from the distorted image of a child of God damaged by the fallen world? We know we are not good BUT it is not about us, it is about God and His will and His purpose. God needs to share His ways and thoughts and purposes with us because He has chosen to involve us in His story.

I have observed that many people who desperately want God to speak to them, give off 'spiritual noise' that is discernible and blocks them from hearing. Shutting the noise off and remembering this is all about who God is and not us helps.

NOTES

HOW DO I DO THAT?
STOP SPIRITUAL NOISE

Spiritual noise seems to come with desperation and activity, a mental frenzy when there is a desire to have connection or to earn favour and it is not happening.

STOP ALL ACTIVITY - Go and sit somewhere in peace and isolation, outside under a tree, beside a stream.

RELAX - just breathe slowly and deeply.

STOP STRIVING - empty your mind. Let your mind be filled with the rhythm of nature around you.

BE EXPECTANT - just be open to God - content to sit beside Him.

JUST BREATHE HIM IN - this is the God of absolute power and absolute goodness.

SEE GOD INVITING YOU INTO HIS STORY - Let him lead, you follow.

Stand in the waterfall of his presence.
THIS IS THE PLACE OF PEACE JESUS GAVE TO US:

> *Peace I leave with you; my peace I give you. I do not give to you as the world gives. Do not let your hearts be troubled and do not be afraid.*
> *John 14:27*

> *In repentance and rest is your salvation, in quietness and trust is your strength.*
> *Isaiah 30:15*

It might take a time or two to be able to let go but persevere.

Let us be clear, because Jesus died on the Cross that we might be cleansed and forgiven for our sin, we can now consciously choose to live in the Waterfall of The Father's presence, in the flow of the

Holy Spirit, aligning ourselves with His will and purpose and putting our trust for all things in Him.

We had lost this in the Fall. The spiritual death that God had predicted if the fruit was eaten came about because we lost the connection to the Father. In the Waterfall we have the environment for continual two-way communication as God the Father intended with His children. There is a flow to conversation, input and responses, questions and answers, humour and reflections. Think how often and in how many ways a father communicates with his children. Indeed the father takes the responsibility to initiate talk on many subjects, in ways that are continually changing as the child grows and matures. Well so it is with God.

If I choose to live my life in the Waterfall GOD WILL COMMUNICATE WITH ME in creative ways to enjoy what we mean to each other, to achieve His purpose. He will continually share what is appropriate for where I am on the journey:

> *He guides the humble in what is right and teaches them His way.*
> *Psalm 25:9*

If He does go silent, seek His perspective. He cannot act outside His character, His silence is not rejection or petulance. He has not left you. He is probably building your spiritual muscle so that you stand on what you believe of Him. Remain trusting in the Waterfall and when He is ready you WILL hear again.

LEVELS OF SHARING

Jesus did not share His insights and thinking equally with everyone whilst He walked the earth. He often spoke with large crowds as in Luke 5:1-10 but they went home at the end of the day. Remaining with Him were four men who *"left everything and followed Him"* Peter, Andrew, James and John. That day on the beach they crossed a line into the unknown, leaving their own world and trusting in Jesus alone, they stepped into a totally new landscape, following where Jesus led.

When Jesus shared a parable with a crowd, after they had left He would often open up further insights to His disciples. Even within the committed twelve disciples there were differences. Jesus did not take all of them up the mountain for the Transfiguration. He had those of an inner circle who were shown more in an intimacy with Jesus, that connected man in the most profound way ever to our God. What were the keys to this? I would suggest trust and commitment.

REVIEW THE WAY YOU COMMUNICATE WITH GOD NOW

When did you last hear from God? Many people think this is a tricky question. Is there some judgement in play here? No there is not, but we often think there is; we feel it is a test. Am I going to be in or out as a Christian, depending on my answer?

Just between you and God, think about how you would sum up the way you talk with Him, is it formal? Stilted? Easy? Flowing? As a servant or as a friend? To someone close or distant? To someone interested in YOU or indifferent? How long ago is it since you felt God spoke to you? Ages past? This year? Today? Sometimes? Often? Never?

Of course, God does speak outside the Waterfall but there is a difference. When we accept Jesus as Saviour, it is as though we become supporters of a football club. The fans may know a lot about the club and dress in all the right gear and attend all the matches but they go home at the end of the match. How different to those who are players, committed to the team, with confidence and trust in the manager. They not only know his mind about the overall strategy of the club but week by week he shares his tactics to overcome the problems the opposing team will present on the next Saturday. Further, the manager has his players whole well-being at heart, their health, diet, and fitness. He is responsible for their training and development as players and will look beyond their playing days to prepare them for the next stage of their journey after football. There has to be continual communication to facilitate all this. The players are there because their desire is to play football and they are prepared to 'live' football as a way of life.

So in part how we communicate with God depends on us, what are we signing up to in our walk with the Lord? How trusting and committed are we?

The good news is that God is there for all of us. Before we know Him He is calling us. Now when we profess Jesus as Lord in our lives and we have the Holy Spirit as a deposit within us, the hearing is easier and if we will step into the Waterfall aligning ourselves to the Father's will and purpose, we are back in the flow of the Holy Spirit where communication is continual.

Deep calls to deep in the roar of your waterfalls. Psalm 42:7

It is the place where you stand to live your life that counts. Are you in? Or are you out? One of the crowd or a disciple? It makes a difference to the relationship.

More good news. You are only ever a step away from being in the Waterfall. All it takes is, *"Sorry God, I do not want to live my life independently of you. Forgive me. I am going to trust you for everything in my life. I want to be aligned to your will and purpose"* and with one step you are back in BECAUSE JESUS DIED SO THE WAY BACK

IS OPEN. There believe what comes into your head and your heart in the Spirit's flow comes from the Father.

WAYS TO HEAR

When God created us for relationship, He gave us the resources and the abilities to share heart to heart with Himself along with all that was necessary to be in tune with Him and to accomplish His purposes through us. Major sources of our understanding come through:

The work of the Holy Spirit
The witness of the Holy Spirit
Creation
Scripture
Other people
Our minds and hearts
Circumstances and events
Direct audible speech
Books and pictures
Visions

This list is not comprehensive, we have an inventive God who will go to great lengths to share creatively with us.

Most Christians are aware of God's touch sometime.

....

I was confirmed in the Anglican church when I was about 14 years old. Not understanding anything about a relational God, I had no understanding of the amazing experience that was mine when the bishop laid his hands on me. I knew something was going on but had no idea what.

It was almost fifty years later when I was journeying in the Waterfall before I recognised what was being imparted to me then. It was the love of the Father. By then I had learned His love language that was previously unknown to me.

....

CHAPTER 7

COME AND SEE

 Often when someone stands on the brink of the Waterfall and it seems very risky for them to step in, I repeat the words of Jesus to two of John the Baptist's disciples:

The next day John was there with two of his disciples.
When he saw Jesus passing by, he said, "Look, the Lamb of God!"
When the two disciples heard him say this, they followed Jesus.
Turning round, Jesus saw them following and asked, "What do you want?"
They said, "Rabbi" (which means Teacher), "where are you staying?"
"Come," he replied, "and you will see."
So they went and saw where he was staying, and spent that day with him.
It was about the tenth hour.
John 1:35-42

What a day this was for these two. John the Baptist proclaims with solid conviction the amazing, awesome truth of who Jesus is and this intrigues and entices them it seems, somewhat tremulously, to follow Him. Jesus, aware of their lurking behind, turns and gently confronts them, *"What do you want?"* Of all the deep and profound things this might have opened up they could only manage a very common place, *"Where are you staying?"*

When Jesus said *"Come and see"*, Jesus was not offering them a view of His sleeping arrangements. He knew what was behind the words and was saying, *"Come, spend time with me and see for yourself what this is all about."* Spending that day in the company of Jesus convinced Andrew to urgently find his brother Simon to tell him, *"We have found the Messiah."* Lives change when people enter into the Waterfall for it is Jesus who beckons, saying, *"Come and see."*

In the Waterfall we are back into the flow of the Holy Spirit and connected to the Father. Jesus lived in this place as He walked on the earth. He believed what came into His head and His heart was from the Father and He OBEYED.

Very wet behind the ears, as a new Christian I was rung up by a concerned lady on the prayer chain. (This allows urgent matters for prayer to be passed quickly round a group of people. Each person having been notified of the need, contacts the next person on the chain.) A young man with a history of mental health problems was travelling from London to stay with someone from the chapel. He had left London hours previously but had not turned up at the station which was on a direct line. Search parties from the church were out looking for him. I put the phone down.

For the first time I sat quietly and asked God where the man was and into my head came the name of a station miles away. I got into my car and drove there. Unsurprised, I found the man sitting outside in the sunshine and took him home where there was much rejoicing.

What did that do for me? I, with the child-like trust of ignorance, had expected God to sort it and He had. It began the building of my faith and trust in God. Next time, I remembered what God had done and stood on that as I took the next step. It has built for me a firm belief that I can trust the character of God. Try it. Jesus is saying "Come and see".

LEARNING TO LISTEN – HEAD AND HEART

Jesus was in constant touch with His Father except so painfully when on the Cross. It was the result of being in His presence, in the Waterfall and we are in that place too. Jesus in the flow of the Spirit did only what His Father gave Him to do, that is He did what came into His head and His heart. Jesus said the words the Father gave Him to say, that is He said the words that came into His head and His heart. We can believe what comes into our head and our heart too.

1996 was a very hard year for me. My husband was dying from cancer and would die on Christmas Eve. We had a difficult relationship as he blamed me for his illness. His days were quite upside down, he would sleep most of the day, drink all evening and be awake most of the night. He needed an increasing amount of nursing and I was very short of sleep, being almost punch drunk with fatigue. I was also working full time, had damaged my back and had children messily battling through to adulthood. I could not cope.

However, it was a very blessed year because I discovered that there was nothing that God would not help me do.

I would get through the day by asking God, "What next?" and I would do what came into my head and heart. I managed all the things that needed to be done. I learned to obey what came into my head and heart and to act on it at once.

One day I went out to a chest freezer we had in an outbuilding. As I opened it I gagged. The electricity must have been off for a long time and the smell coming from it was choking. There was a mound of rotting meat in it. I dropped the lid and leaned back against the wall. The prospect of dealing with this was too appalling, too overwhelming. I could not do it. Into my head came, "Go and get the hose." With the obedience I had learned, I automatically went for the hose pipe. "Go and put it in the freezer." As I was walking back I began to realise what I was doing. This was crazy! I put the hosepipe into the freezer. "Now go and turn the tap on." Everything within me was fighting. What was I doing? A voice in my head was screaming, "This is making it worse!" but I had learned to obey, so I did it. After some time "Turn the tap off. Go and get a bottle of bleach." I did so. "Pour it into the freezer." When holding my nose I gingerly opened the freezer. The water had just covered the contents and I emptied the bleach in as quickly as possible and slammed the lid shut. "That's it for today." Mystified, but thankful, I retreated.

It was three days later that into my head came, "Time for the freezer!" I cannot describe how little I wanted to face this problem. I would have left it much longer!!!!! Cautiously, I approached the freezer and inched the lid open but what a surprise. NO SMELL! To me it was incredible, the freezer was full of grey sludge but no smell! After that it was easy to empty it with a bucket. Job done.

Never in a million years, if I had been on the best form possible, would I have thought of doing what I did, so what was going on here? God was teaching me on so many levels. It was the early days of my learning how to live in the Waterfall. I had learned to trust and to obey, believing that what came into my head and heart came through the direct flow of the Holy Spirit sharing God's heart. This allowed all the creativity of Our Living God to flow into my daily life. I tell this story because if God in all His might and majesty cares enough to stoop and help me with a stinky freezer, will He not care about you and me and be trustworthy with the things that concern us deeply?

One of the things you might have noticed was the way God spoke, giving directions in short easy steps, which took account of exactly where I was at that time. It sometimes is a concern to people that they might not hear when God speaks but you can be confident that when you have committed to living in the Waterfall God has your training programme mapped out so that you will accomplish all He has for you to do. He needs you to hear.

I have heard people say with disparagement that God is not there to find parking spaces. My experience is exactly the opposite. Nothing is too small for His concern. I could fill this book and more with examples.

It was my custom to take my Dad and Mum on holiday in the last few years they were together, not I hasten to add as a chore but because we enjoyed each other and had fun together. In May we would book a cottage for a week and our days fell into a contented pattern. We would go out in the morning taking a flask of coffee, to wander the highways and byways searching for beauty and interest for Mum to sketch. One of the reasons we had fun was the lively way Mum and Dad observed the world. We might lunch out, then go back to rest during the afternoon before taking a picnic and finding some seaside vantage point to while away the evening.

In the last couple of years in their late eighties, they were both quite frail and I would ask Jesus to come too and He in very real and practical ways got involved in the details of the holiday. Crossing roads, two people were needed to look out for Mum and Dad, there were two, Him and me. When out for drives I would ask Him for things to delight, parking spaces with views, loos when we needed. It was a joint effort.

On the last holiday, Mum who had been quite poorly for some time needed some new clothes. She had lost weight and for some time had not been able to go shopping to a British Homes Store which she liked because they had small sizes that suited her. From home the journey was too much for her by then. We were near Exeter and I suddenly felt we should see if there was a BHS there. We drove into the city. I had not been there before but I did what came into my head and my heart. I ignored several signs to car parks and then saw one I knew was 'it'. I zoomed in, ignored the disabled bays, where normally we would stop because Mum had mobility difficulties, up three full floors, round a corner into a free space next to a door into the shopping mall. Through the door on the right was BHS and by the door was the petite ladies' clothes section, so, within fifty feet of the car, we bought all Mum needed. Please do not tell me this was coincidence. I know what was happening here. Shopping done, there faced us a delightful but very busy cafe with just the one table - perfect for us to have lunch. Thank you, Lord.

If this stretches your credibility *"Come and see."* I have found God eager to be involved in every part of our lives, nothing is too small or insignificant for Him. Is this frivolous? No it certainly is not. These experiences convinced me that I had stepped into God's world where nothing was beyond Him and that there was a robust reality to His wonderful, beautiful, loving character that is thankfully all about Him and not me.

Let us just be clear what I mean by God speaking to us. I mean any method that God chooses that lets me know what is on His heart.

AN AUDIBLE VOICE

God has a voice that is undeniable; once heard, without any doubt you know it is God. There is biblical evidence that God can speak audibly. Many seem to think that was for Biblical times but not for now. My experience is different.

One of the first times I heard Him speak was when the house was on fire. During the afternoon I had smelt a whiff of singeing when I had been in the bathroom but I had assumed it was a bonfire from the coal yard next door. It was a common thing but I looked around upstairs. There was nothing out of the ordinary.

I went back to the other end of the house, engrossed in what I was doing. After another hour I heard loudly "Fire!" I knew God's voice so now I knew to act. I ran up stairs and woke my husband. There was some smoke but no fire. Downstairs out of the back door and it was obvious from the glow that the fire was in my son's room.

The fire started in the room we had built onto the five hundred year old cottage and therefore, was of modern construction. It began because a faulty wire from a bedside lamp was lying across bedding. The fire officer said that it had smouldered for hours and only at the last moment had it burst into flame. If it had broken through into the old part of the house it would have spread very rapidly. He was of the opinion that my husband might not have got out. As it was, the room was devastated; the house was not.

On reflection, I realised that I had been uneasy all afternoon but I had rationalised the disquiet, persuading myself that all was well and ignoring the disturbance of my peace. That afternoon God was using two ways to alert me. The disturbance of my peace I learnt means that there is something of which I need to be aware. My immediate question now would be, "What do I need to see here Lord?" and I would lift my head and use all my senses to explore what I needed to understand. When I missed the signal and remained unaware of danger God took action that I would not ignore - He spoke.

JESUS – THE ROMANCE

As with any meaningful relationship, we develop a growing awareness of the other person, we read the signals, we send messages so that bonds and understanding between us are deepened. In each relationship that matters to you there will be a unique template of communication that is the foundation for the togetherness you enjoy. So it is with God.

You know His voice. We have looked at some direct ways God has spoken but He leads you deeper!

I wanted a third marriage. Now I was a Christian I wanted to do it right, I had made such a mess of two! I wanted to honour God by having a 'Christian marriage' and I really wanted an intimate relationship that was not destructive. Other widows around me were finding new companions and I was asking God, "When will it be my turn?" He made it clear this path was not for me because He wanted to be my husband. That took the wind from my sails and set off many conflicting emotions within me, from awe to anger but mostly it was confusion. Just what did it mean?

It was the start of a new phase of my life with Jesus that continues to take my breath away. However, it began with a ring. I was on holiday with a close friend and I came down one morning after my quiet time knowing that I needed to go and buy an engagement ring. We quested most of the day before, in a very small coastal village in Suffolk, I found THE one. Sometimes I have living HD movies in my mind and spirit that I am part of and that night Jesus came and took me to meet the Father and the Holy Spirit, as a man might introduce his prospective bride to his family. Their reactions I hold within me and confirm for me the awesome reality which is true for us all. GOD LOVES US.

However, not long after I was at a wedding and there was dancing. Afterwards I shared with Jesus, somewhat petulantly, that it was all right being engaged to

Him but no-one has ever wanted to dance with me. The next time I was in church worshipping, He came and asked me to dance. Since then we have danced in ballrooms, amongst the stars and on hillsides, all the dances you can think of and some more, and I have to tell you that Jesus is a radical dancer!

I told no-one of this but not long afterwards I was on a course and communion was being passed along the row. I sat at the end and the lady next to me offered me the bread and then as she turned back she said over her shoulder, "By the way Jesus says He loves the dancing."

Over the next two years I learnt much about being in a relationship and about being looked after, for if Jesus was indeed going to be my husband not only did I have to let Him have His place but I needed Him to deliver. He increased the ways I knew to get specific and detailed answers from Him.

I learned I could trust Him on new levels and whatever I was facing He was present to walk with me through it. I was still adjusting to this when I had the next romantic crisis. Okay, Valentine's Day may be commercialism's take on romance but I had never been made to feel special on that day or in that way. So when I had been with many people revelling in their chocolates and flowers I, in my emptiness, started grumbling on the way home in the car. "I do not get anything on Valentine's Day."

Jesus said, "But I did all this for you. Look out of the window." Outside it was a very frosty February day and I was driving through the Sussex lanes of great beauty in late afternoon sunlight. It was stunning. He said, "I did this for you." You see something of His scale in this: they got a bunch of flowers, I got Sussex transformed. It is hard to find the words that describe how special and loved and connected I felt. My wish, just because it was MY wish, was important to Jesus.

I learnt something else. All day, when I had been wanting I had looked with envy on others. As soon as I turned and faced Jesus and spoke to Him, albeit petulantly, the door was open for Him to provide for my wish to be fulfilled. This relationship is not just about His providing for me but delighting and surprising me, with abundance and thoughtfulness. Now I know to turn my face to Him sooner and know that He has the answers I need and the ways to make my life special with Him.

Since that Valentine's Day Jesus has not missed bringing me a gift on that day. Sometimes again He does it directly, sometimes He sends people. One day by 10.45pm there was still nothing. Preparing to go to bed I said to Him, "It's OK Lord I know you love me. It's just chocolates would have been nice." There was a knock on my locked back door and my daughter arrived with a heart shaped box of chocolates, "Sorry Mum, I forgot these earlier."

One day I was away working at a church over a weekend and the colleague I was working with arrived on the Sunday, which was the 14th, and called me over to his car. He opened the boot and took out some flowers. He said he was driving along and God told him, " Go and buy the girl a bunch of flowers." So he did. Jesus has not missed one Valentine's Day and He will never do so because it matters to me.

....

Everything in this book is about knowing God and being known as we journey with Him. He is growing my character as I explore His; He is sharing the fullness of who He is, as He makes me into the creation He designed me to be.
WHAT A LOVE STORY.

NOTES

CHAPTER 8

WAYS AND MEANS

In Isaiah there are some profound words which I believe are very significant for disciples :

I am the Lord, who has made all things, who alone stretched out the heavens, who spread out the earth by myself. Isaiah 44:24

... who carries out the words of his servants and fulfils the predictions of his messengers. Isaiah 44:26

The journey we have been speaking of takes the disciple from being damaged and untutored, where obedience and trust are needed to build faith, through to maturity. There in the flow of the Holy Spirit and having learned to work in the plans and purposes of God, He then honours us by trusting us to take the initiative, just as He trusted Adam within His plans to name the animals.

This part of Isaiah for me shows the circle. God Almighty *"spread out the earth"* BY HIMSELF but He then closes the loop by carrying out the words of His servants because in His story He has chosen to use us His children to fulfil His works.

One of the most exciting things is watching fledglings grow through from uncertain flappings to confident flight, from a place of uncertainty as they fledge, to flying confidently with fully extended wings . On our journey it is only possible for us to extend ourselves and to be all we were designed to be if we are trusted and given space to launch ourselves forth. Ultimately, on this Waterfall journey God honours us with that space having trained us into His ways.

We can influence what actually happens. God revealed how writing things down can be significant in this:

I was in Serbia, part of a team that regularly went out to Temerin, north of Novi Sad. We were out for over three weeks and one weekend we had a visitor at lunch in the home of the Ivan and Zorica where we stayed. His name was Alan, an American who had driven for two days with a car load of shoes destined for the local gypsy population and would, after lunch, drive back to the UK.

As we were sitting round the circular table eating he told us that he had brought us a message from the Holy Spirit. As I take my mind back there, I can still feel the shimmering power as Alan delivered it.

Up to six months previously he had been living in the USA but had wanted to take up a position as part of a team decommissioning a nuclear reactor in Kent. He was thwarted at every turn by red tape and his inability to sell a property. He was frustrated and perplexed because he felt God was calling him to the UK.

Alan attended a local conference where the main speaker was Dr. Paul Yonggi Cho the pastor of the world's largest church in Seoul, South Korea. His message that day was entitled 'Write it down'.

Dr. Cho knew God was calling him to be a pastor but he was struggling with where to start. God told him to write down what he needed to begin, so he wrote down a bike and a desk. God told him to be more specific so the colour and make of the bike went down and detail of the desk he envisaged.

The next day he went out in the city to see someone, and there outside, leaning against the wall was THE bike. He said nothing, concluded his business and went home. Then he had a call, the man had forgotten to ask him if he would like the bike? Next day he was elsewhere and spoke to a man who was sitting at THE desk. He was offered that, too and then the doors swung open for him to begin his ministry.

Alan left the conference and began his list of everything he needed to make the move to the UK happen. Within two weeks every blockage was removed and two months later he was in England. Only one thing remained on his list. He had written his wish that the position he was to fulfil might be upgraded to management level; within days of his beginning work this was done.

It was a powerful message, powerfully delivered. It felt so important that God had sent Alan on a four day trip across Europe for us to hear it. The impact it had on me was profound and I am continually putting it into practice. I have come to believe writing it down is one of the ways God allows us to co-operate in His purposes.

THINGS TO LEARN

Knowing it was God's heart I started at once.

I began by creating specific and detailed lists of expectations, which I kept in a special journal, for each of the different areas of my life that were important to me – family, ministry, trips and particular situations. Amazing things began to happen. I began ticking off the things that came into being. So I began to think bigger and I would write down the best I could imagine but God kept exceeding my expectations. So I began to think bigger.

The last time I went with Pam to Uganda we did our lists, four sides of A4 paper filled with expectations for the trip, about travel and what we were leaving behind in the UK; about our wellbeing and comfort, our growth and anointing; about relationships, our ministry, working together, opportunities to make a difference; about growth for the kingdom, the fruit to come and the blessings to flow. I had been regularly to Uganda and it seemed that all those visits were preparation for this one. When we came back, every one of those items were not only ticked off but blown away.

What have I learned of God through this? Firstly, we have a BIG God who is daring us to think bigger. My experience is of the Father hugely enjoying exceeding the best I can think or imagine. As we were at the airport coming home from Entebbe, reflecting in awe at what had been achieved, at the checkout we were given the final flourish. "Oh ladies, we are upgrading you." Have you heard God laugh? The journey home was a delicious pampering in the warm glow of His presence.

Secondly, I have learned that God wants my involvement because it is the way He has chosen to work. James 4:2 tells it starkly:

You do not have because you do not ask God.

However, in the Waterfall in the flow of the spirit there is an alignment "the deep calling to deep", where God joys in our involvement and revels in our trust. Here our aligning ourselves to His will and purpose because He has chosen this way, allows Him to throw open doors and make things happen on an unimaginable scale.

Thirdly, the timing is God's. Some things take longer than others, sometimes years pass but I know what is on the list is in play. The outcomes are frequently off the scale and may not be what I expect but I always know that "they will work together for good", because my list, prepared in the flow of the Holy Spirit, is "serving His purposes".

Fourthly, there was no doubt in those of us sitting at that lunch table in Serbia that God was giving us a tool He wanted us to use. In obeying and seeing what God has done through it, He has grown my faith step by step and revealed Himself in glorious and surprising ways.

Let Dr. Yonggi Cho say it again, **"Write it down!"** and remember that he runs the largest church in the world with some 800,000 members. I hear our God laughing with delight again.

NOTES

_____

_____

_____

_____

_____

_____

_____

_____

_____

_____

HOW DO I DO THAT?
WRITE IT DOWN

1. BE IN THE WATERFALL OF GOD'S PRESENCE and in a book write down what you would like to see in each area of your life – be specific, think big. (A book is good because you can look back and check on progress over time.)

2. THINK – Going to a conference? Systematically, think through what it will entail: planning, travel, accommodation, teaching, growth, worship and write down the best and biggest agenda for each area that comes into your head. THEN THINK BIGGER!

3. EXPECT and BELIEVE that God will do this and more.

4. LEARN WITH GOD – this is one of the main ways I have learnt something about God's perspectives. Review what has happened. Give thanks for the answers. Learn from what has been done. Tune in and watch God work His purposes out as He unfolds the outworking of the lists. The character of God becomes real and living as He does so and His desire to be involved with us has a dynamic expression.

5. ENJOY WORKING AND BEING INVOLVED WITH THE WILD EXTRAVAGANCE OF OUR LAVISH GOD.

This is **THE** adventure.

There are different ways for God to reveal His heart to us that involve pen and paper:

Write down the revelation and make it plain on tablets so that a herald may run with it. Habakkuk 2:2

This is seen very powerfully in David's life. When he at last was established in Jerusalem he wanted to build a temple for the Lord. He was told that he was not the one to do the building, Solomon his son would have this responsibility but as he was young and inexperienced David would do the preparations.

"All this," David said, "I have in writing from the hand of the Lord upon me and he gave me understanding in all the details of the plan."
1 Chronicles 28:19

David not only understood the building and all the resources needed but where they would come from. He knew what articles and furniture would be needed and how the temple would run. David, touched by the Spirit, knew when God wanted to share the vision and he sat down and facilitated it.

In the early days of my walk I was fed by reading *"God Calling"* by *The Two Listeners*. The two women who wrote the book chose to remain anonymous. Each day they sat with paper and pen. It was 1932 and they just waited on God, then wrote down what He gave them. The result is a remarkable devotional.

Have you ever tried doing the same? It is amazing. Just sit down with pen and paper and be in His presence. Write down what comes into your head and your heart. In my experience, often I only have a word but as soon as I put pen to paper the words flow. Some of the revelations are for me and some have wider application or are thoughts on world issues. Doing it daily for a period is especially illuminating.

THE SILENCE OF GOD

I am sure that some people are thinking that I should get 'real' because God does not always speak to us in a loud, clear voice and sometimes He leaves us for periods with no word from Himself. I would agree but I would also say those times too are telling us something of His purposes.

Firstly, we are all on a journey. When we step into full discipleship in the Waterfall, God needs to speak more to us to train and heal us, we are His chosen vessels. To begin with He will be very clear, give us small steps and clear directions but as we go on He will vary the way He speaks. The first time He uses the still, small voice it takes faith to believe and step out on that alone. However, God has a distinctive voice, just as you and I have, and we can know that voice so that whether it is a whisper or a shout we will obey. As you move on, it is the character of God that becomes the certainty within you. God is good and cannot act outside His character so when circumstances look bleak YOU KNOW you can trust God and can stand on His Word.

Secondly, in His silence He is training us to stand on what we believe, to stand on who He is, whether we feel His presence or not. He is growing us from being privates in the army where we just have to obey orders, up through the ranks and as we become more involved and know the commander's mind better we are able to operate independently. However, because we are in tune with Him in that independence, we will be able to act and speak His words as though He were present. The aim in training soldiers is to produce fit, well-balanced individuals who are welded into a unit. Along the way they are given the skills to serve, to learn how the army operates and how to play their part. Also, there is much emphasis on them personally, on their fitness and character. Soldiers go on exercise to build up combat readiness. They are put into situations they are likely to face in battle to build confidence and trust and muscle. **SOMETIMES GOD GOES QUIET TO BUILD OUR SPIRITUAL MUSCLE.**

Thirdly, in silence God is opening up our awareness of ourselves and the different layers of spiritual activity around us, for as disciples we must see beyond and beneath the surface of worldly activity.

I used to be in the Police Force many years ago. I learnt very quickly there were different layers of life all occupying the same space but not interconnecting. There was an ordinary, normal, law abiding strata and then there were layers of villainy and poverty and homelessness. As a police constable you had to tune into the right sub-culture to see what was going on.

HOW DO I DO THAT?
UNDERSTAND THE MIND OF GOD

STOP AND STAND BACK – quieten any spiritual noise and activity. Often when God goes quiet our response is to panic about what have we done wrong, "I knew it. I am not worthy." But look at the bigger picture. Believe God has not gone away, so why is this happening? STAND IN THE WATERFALL – with your face towards the Father, remembering this is the place of TRUST.

EVERYTHING STARTS WITH GOD – and who He really is. He cannot act outside His character and He is building a people of power. As we journey, the landscape is constantly changing, but it is not random; we are following the path that God needs us to travel for us to fulfil our unique role for Him.

DETACH AND STAND BACK – when we are in the middle of a situation it is hard to understand all the dynamics, we can be just too close to see and understand. I picture Jesus standing on a hill with me beside Him, like a General looking down on a battlefield with His staff. Often talking it through with another objective and spiritually sensitive person is very helpful.

ASK THE QUESTION OF JESUS – Please show me what is going on.
Disciples need to be seeking to see what God sees:

> *When the servant of the man of God got up and went out early the next morning, an army with horses and chariots had surrounded the city. "Oh no, my lord! What shall we do?" the servant asked. "Don't be afraid," the prophet answered. "Those who are with us are more than those who are with them." And Elisha prayed, "Open his eyes, Lord, so that he may see." Then the Lord opened the servant's eyes, and he looked and saw the hills full of horses and chariots of fire all around Elisha.*
> *2 Kings 6:15 - 17*

The disciples also asked the same question of Jesus many times:

> When He was alone, the Twelve and others
> around him asked him about the parables.
> Mark 4:10

Jesus on that occasion took the time to give them further insights about the parable of the Sower. Disciples NEED the inside story!
Indeed in Amos it says:

> Surely the Sovereign Lord does nothing without
> revealing his plan to his servants the prophets.
> Amos 3:7

IN TIMES OF TROUBLE – Now my question is, "Lord where are you in this? Please help me see what you see." I choose to trust and claim His peace because this is where everything works together for good for those who love the Lord and serve His purposes. The General is still in command and will share with you what He needs you to understand at this time.

DAILY HABIT – Ask not only when you are baffled or want deeper insight but make it a habit so you are always looking for God's perspective. Silence and seasons, valleys and dark places will not last forever, only until we have learned or experienced that which is needful. Working with God towards understanding advances the Kingdom. God is seeking intelligent co-operation in His plans and as we gradually learn to have 'the mind of Christ' seeing what He sees, thinking His way, God trusts us more and more.

> "For my thoughts are not your thoughts, neither
> are your ways my ways," declares the Lord.
> Isaiah 55 : 8

Some things are not ours to know but He has created us to be family, insiders in His plans and purposes and to that end and to that measure His thinking is open to us.

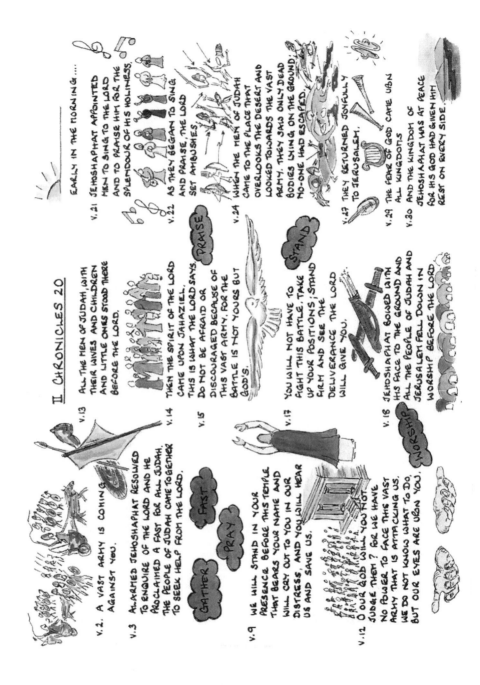

II CHRONICLES 20

v.2. A VAST ARMY IS COMING AGAINST YOU.

v.3 ALARMED JEHOSHAPHAT RESOLVED TO ENQUIRE OF THE LORD AND HE PROCLAIMED A FAST FOR ALL JUDAH. THE PEOPLE OF JUDAH CAME TOGETHER TO SEEK HELP FROM THE LORD.

GATHER
FAST
PRAY

v.9 WE WILL STAND IN YOUR PRESENCE BEFORE THIS TEMPLE THAT BEARS YOUR NAME AND WILL CRY OUT TO YOU IN OUR DISTRESS, AND YOU WILL HEAR US AND SAVE US.

v.12 O OUR GOD WILL YOU NOT JUDGE THEM? FOR WE HAVE NO POWER TO FACE THIS VAST ARMY THAT IS ATTACKING US. WE DO NOT KNOW WHAT TO DO, BUT OUR EYES ARE UPON YOU.

v.13 ALL THE MEN OF JUDAH, WITH THEIR WIVES AND CHILDREN AND LITTLE ONES STOOD THERE BEFORE THE LORD.

v.14 THEN THE SPIRIT OF THE LORD CAME UPON JAHAZIEL,

v.15 THIS IS WHAT THE LORD SAYS, DO NOT BE AFRAID OR DISCOURAGED BECAUSE OF THIS VAST ARMY, FOR THE BATTLE IS NOT YOURS BUT GOD'S.

PRAISE

STAND

v.17 YOU WILL NOT HAVE TO FIGHT THIS BATTLE. TAKE UP YOUR POSITIONS; STAND FIRM AND SEE THE DELIVERANCE THE LORD WILL GIVE YOU.

v.18 JEHOSHAPHAT BOWED WITH HIS FACE TO THE GROUND AND ALL THE PEOPLE OF JUDAH AND JERUSALEM FELL DOWN IN WORSHIP BEFORE THE LORD

WORSHIP

EARLY IN THE MORNING....

v.21 JEHOSHAPHAT APPOINTED MEN TO SING TO THE LORD AND TO PRAISE HIM FOR THE SPLENDOUR OF HIS HOLINESS;

v.22 AS THEY BEGAN TO SING AND PRAISE, THE LORD SET AMBUSHES;

v.24 WHEN THE MEN OF JUDAH CAME TO THE PLACE THAT OVERLOOKS THE DESERT AND LOOKED TOWARDS THE VAST ARMY, THEY SAW ONLY DEAD BODIES LYING ON THE GROUND; NO-ONE HAD ESCAPED.

v.27 THEY RETURNED JOYFULLY TO JERUSALEM,

v.29 THE FEAR OF GOD CAME UPON ALL KINGDOMS

v.30 AND THE KINGDOM OF JEHOSHAPHAT WAS AT PEACE FOR HIS GOD HAD GIVEN HIM REST ON EVERY SIDE.

ENQUIRING OF GOD

Sometimes we need answers that are more than just one thought. The day before I needed to know God's mind in detail, I had been reading about David in the Old Testament. When David needed direction from God about a course of action he would 'enquire of the Lord'. He did it seven times and in each case he would then know what was coming and his part in it. Other prophets too enquired of the Lord and in the flow of the Holy Spirit could speak out God's thinking in great detail. If that happened in the Old Testament, I reflected how much more should that be open to us who have the Holy Spirit in and with us. I always believe that if God gives me an insight I am to use it and the opportunity quickly follows. It did!

In July 2006 there was a call on the answering machine from Judith. Would I come to Nepal next February to do a People Helpers' Biblical counselling course in Kathmandhu and Pokhara?

In the past I had been terrified to cross the English Channel, mainly because I suffered very badly from travel sickness but in 2001 God had told me to have my bags packed and to go where He sent me. I could write another book about the consequences, suffice it to say here that it was the beginning of an international ministry for me.

However, my first reaction to the thought of Nepal was apprehension for many reasons: because of the political instability in Nepal - there had been recent reports of violence with the Maoists; because of the altitude - knowing how susceptible I had been to sickness when both feet were not on flat ground; because of such a long haul flight - I had never been that far; because it was to be a very small plane on the flight from Kathmandu to Pokhara, skirting the Himalayas but mainly because I was just scared if I went I would not come back.

So I said that I would enquire of the Lord to see if it was right for me to go. At that moment I hoped the answer would be no. As I went to bed I simply said, "Lord I am enquiring of you, do I go to Nepal?"

The following morning I got God's answer. The double page of UCB's Word for Today had confirmations that fairly leapt out at me.

There was a heading, 'You'll get through it.' Life will either bury you or bless you; the difference lies in your having the right attitude, "in all these things we are more than conquerors." Romans 8: 37

The second heading was, 'Putting God's kingdom first.'

What does it mean to put God first in your life? There followed a list of 12 things and these stood out for me:- Obedience to God – Anyone who obeys God's laws and teaches them will be great in the kingdom of heaven. Matthew 5:19

Faith in God – If you had faith as small as a mustard seed and nothing would be impossible .... but with God everything is possible. Matthew 17:20 and Matthew 19:26

Blessing people – *Jesus not only taught this but His constant healing of, training and serving others demonstrated how to do it.*

Disciple making – *Therefore go and make disciples of all the nations. Matthew 28:19*

According to Jesus that's the only agenda worth living for and, if necessary, dying for.

Surrendered – *If any one of you wants to be my follower you must put aside your selfish ambition, shoulder your Cross and follow me." Matthew 16:24*

Be resolute – *Blessed is the man whose confidence is in Him. Jeremiah 17:7*

When you have heard from God be resolute, remind yourself that God has given you the grace to succeed at whatever He has called you to do. God's word says, "If you will listen diligently to the voice of the Lord your God you shall be above only and you shall not be beneath." Deuteronomy 28:1&13

Do what God prompts you to do and be resolute about it!

These readings summed up the way I viewed my life with the Lord and gave me the absolute certainty that I must go. Then I did the readings for that day from the Celtic Daily Prayer book, which included :-

... and may you live to see your children's children. Psalm 128:6

To rescue us from the hand of our enemies and to enable us to serve Him without fear. Luke 1:74

And you, my child, will be called a prophet of the Most High: for you will go on before the Lord to prepare the way for Him, to give his people the knowledge of salvation through the forgiveness of their sins, because of the tender mercy of our God, by which the rising sun will come to us from heaven to shine on those living in darkness and in the shadow of death, to guide our feet into the path of peace. Luke 1:76 – 79

Then I will purify the lips of the peoples that all of them may call on the name of the Lord and serve him shoulder to shoulder. Zephaniah 3:9

The Lord the King of Israel is with you never again will you fear any harm. Zephaniah 3:15b

The Lord your God is with you He is mighty to save. He will take great delight in you He will quiet you with his love He will rejoice over you with singing. Zephaniah 3:17

"At that time I will gather you, at that time I will bring you home I will give you honour and praise among all the peoples of the earth when I restore your fortunes before your very eyes," says the Lord. Zephaniah 3:20

In these readings which leapt out at me — not only did God give me the clear indication to go to Nepal but also the absolute assurance that He was in it, and that if I obeyed and followed Jesus that He would bless the work. He also dealt with my fears, encouraged me and gave me intimate glimpses of how He recognised my particular concerns. Finally, He gave me a wonderful insight into the way He viewed me and what we should do together "shoulder to shoulder".
I rang and said yes.

I went to Nepal with the confidence that I was going out at God's side to do His will and that He had everything covered and that it would be fruitful. I have been three times with the same team and have seen God do amazing things through amazing people out there. We took the seeds of the Waterfall Journey and God has used others with their gifts to bring in a harvest in that land.

HOW DO I DO THAT?
ENQUIRE OF THE LORD

1. When in need of complex answers the last thing at night I simply state is *"I enquire of you Lord ..."* and add just a simple question, such as *"Do I go?"*
2. Be expectant of receiving an answer. God can be creative in the ways He communicates this to you.
   However, predominately, but not exclusively, I find His answers in this channel of communication come from His Word.
3. Write down anything from anywhere that stands out to you during the day.
4. Review what you have been given, believe and obey.
5. Every time I have asked in this way I have received the answers I have needed to act upon.

THE SEARCH FOR MEANING

We saw earlier on that one of the CRUCIAL NEEDS we have as image bearers is to see meaning in who we are and what we do. The truth is that unless we stand inside

God's meaning flowing in the Waterfall we will have a yearning emptiness within us. We have been exploring ways to search for God's meaning in many of the elements of discipleship we have so far covered. Finding God's meaning in situations and circumstances, recording and reflecting on the revelations deepens and enriches our unique experience and understanding of our God. It helps us know who we are in the way that Jesus understood who He was and which allowed Him to walk this earth with authority.

I remember Robin Ray, the son of a famous comic Ted Ray talking of his marriage. He and his wife intentionally created memories and planted tangible representations of them as foundation stones, defining the significance and meaning of the relationship they shared.

The more we explore God's meaning the richer we become. Below are one or two creative ways to explore God's meaning for us and for our lives.

REFLECTION

ACTIVITY 1:
Find poems or Bible passages that that are meaningful to you and record them. There are several I illustrated and made into cards to keep with me that are illustrated in this book. I give prayer cards from the nuns of the Carmelite Monastery in Norwich to all participants on courses. Each is an individual message through a picture and a verse from the Father to His child and they have extraordinary impact.

ACTIVITY 2:
On a Spiritual Direction course we spent ten minutes tearing out bits from a pile of assorted magazines that spoke to us of any aspect of God. We then had ten minutes to paste them onto an A3 sheet of paper. The way this was done by each individual spoke volumes about their character and preferences. Mine was a random collection of ragged edged cuttings but it was so powerful I had it on my bedroom wall for four years. It fed me in many ways that drew me deeper into my relationship with God.

ACTIVITY 3:
To explore what is important between you and God either:
Draw a shape that is meaningful for you – it might be a treasure chest or a boat or a rucksack.
Draw the things that you seek or wish to carry as you journey with your God. Add to it as you travel. Ponder the contents.

ACTIVITY 4:
Have a box and collect things that speak of your relationship with God.
Some of my treasures are pen and paper, a tiny Bible, an fish eagle, a paint brush, a feather, a stone from Galilee, a red heart, a picture of Machhapuchre - a mountain in the Himalayas, a grizzly bear and many more. They all speak to me of who God is personally for me and God speaks through them.

He found them in a desert land
in an empty howling wasteland
He surrounded them and watched over them
He guided them as his most precious possession
like an eagle that rouses her chicks
and hovers over her young
So he spreads his wings to take them in
and carried them aloft on his pinions
The Lord alone guided them
they lived without any foreign gods
He made them ride over the highlands
he let them feast on the crops of the fields
He nourished them with honey from the cliffs
with olive oil from the hard rock

Deuteronomy 32:10-13

PART 4

SPIRITUAL MILESTONES ALONG THE WAY

CHAPTER 9

THINGS TO LEARN ABOUT GOD

 In this section I would invite you to walk with me through the spiritual landscape that I have travelled. This journey, of course, is unique for each one of us, nevertheless, there are common aspects that will be important to us all as we take up God's offer to join Him in His story. This is not a theological treatise, it is a personal testimony about the things that mattered to me in deepening the special relationship with each person of the Trinity.

THE WORD OF GOD

I was blessed because the church God put me in after my dramatic conversion had sound, Holy Spirit inspired teaching. Looking back I can clearly see God's tailor-made programme for me to learn and grow in His Word. Especially at the beginning EVERY thing I heard was JUST for me. What a God! Every sermon was just what I needed to hear. I spent the first six months crying my way through each service as God talked personally to me, feeding me comfort and hope. I learnt that if I needed God to speak to me I had only to open my Bible.

I was fortunate that my teachers gave me a love of the Old Testament as well as the New and an appreciation of the importance of both in delivering an understanding of God's story. There is great value in books other than the Bible, indeed my journey, like yours I expect, has been seasoned with several very significant books without which at specific times I would not have made the progress I did, but not at the expense of reading the Bible.

THE FUNDAMENTAL TRUTH is that God is inviting us to enter into His story and thus we need to know about it. On this journey the Bible, the Word of God, all of it, Old and New Testaments is vital.

One of the most startling changes I found in living in the Waterfall was that the Bible came alive in new ways. The Holy Spirit continually broke open the Word and the familiar again and again became extraordinary, mysterious and challenging. The vividness of the lessons the Holy Spirit drew for me from its pages and the revelation that God IS who He says He is and means what He says, altered my journey radically.

God's plan is to grow you, equip you and heal you as He draws you close and into an intimate relationship with Himself. His Word is a constant source of what He has in mind for you NOW. Trust the Holy Spirit will enlighten you. The more you explore His Word the more opportunity God has to share His heart with you.

BIBLE KNOWLEDGE

Today if you ask a group of people to get out their Bibles, many will bring forth a gadget on which they have instant access on the screen before them to any passage, in a choice of versions. This is great for being out and about but your own Bible becomes so much more. Having a book, learning how it is put together, where things are, interacting with the pages, adding notes and colour allows the book to grow into a treasury underpinning your walk. Do have access to the Word in as many ways as possible but I would encourage you not to exclude a handful of book!

HOW DO I DO THAT?
ACQUIRE BIBLICAL KNOWLEDGE

BUY A BIBLE – choose a translation that is accessible for you. There are some great translations. Research, read a few and find one that is good for you.

CREATE A HABIT – at a regular time and in an appropriate place read a few verses from the one book of the Bible. It also helps to know how you learn best. I find colour and notes in margins and pictures help me interact with the content.

Expect the Holy Spirit to speak to you through it. Believe what comes into your head and your heart. Record it and think about it. Do you need to respond?

FIND TEACHING THAT SPEAKS TO YOU – preaching, CDs, podcasts, bible studies.

EXPECT THE HOLY SPIRIT to lead you in your choice of reading plans, daily devotionals and books.
- Ask Him to help you understand what you are reading.
- Watch what comes across your path.
- Tune into the leading of the Holy Spirit ie tune into what you are sensing inside, if it feels right choose that.

READ THROUGH THE WHOLE BIBLE

KEEP A SPIRITUAL JOURNAL

We cannot all go to Bible College but we all have the Holy Spirit Himself available to teach us and give us a revelation of the mind of God.

WHO IS GOD?

One of my first difficulties after being saved was that I was very confused about God. Who is He?

I was an Anglican in my youth. I loved the church which was approached by a long avenue of trees and stood on an escarpment above a river. It was beautiful throughout the seasons. The church was old, of mellow stone and imbued with holiness.

I loved the church, I loved the liturgy and the atmosphere and I loved the sun coming through the stained glass windows. Through my teens I went to communion three times a week. I was confirmed after six months of classes and looking back I knew something had happened in that service but I did not know what. I went to a Church of England Teacher Training College but God was not there.

No-one ever opened up for me that there was a relationship on offer. Despite my thinking that I was a Christian, I believed attending church was enough and I ran my life, my way without God's involvement. When things got tough in my twenties and my conscience would not shut up I told the God I knew to get out of my life. It was only when I was forty-six, when I got to the end of me, that I dramatically met Jesus and entered into a relationship with the living God.

So who is this God I need to get to know? The Bible starts *"In the beginning God"* and there follows the glory that is Creation coming into being as God speaks. That is power! God was there before the beginning. His omniscience, His omnipotence, and His omnipresence are beyond our comprehension. Again we learn from the Bible that *"His ways are not our ways and His thoughts are not our thoughts"*. In profound perfection and absolute power our holy God reigns in majesty.

However, God is also about relationships. His character is the foundation of all His purposes. He is a unit of three persons in one, with love and harmony being His essence. The nature of love is that it needs to be shared and so God created human beings to be His children. God created us in love, in His image with free will because He wanted a family who would choose to return His love and trust.

THE FAMILY LIKENESS

When God created man, he made him in the likeness of God. He created them male and female and blessed them. Genesis 5:1

What does God see when He looks at us? This clearly states we are image bearers of God himself. That is an amazing, exciting truth. As I write this we are expecting a new baby boy to be added to our family. The anticipation, the wondering, the longing to meet the new arrival is felt throughout the family.

I already have four grandsons and each one is precious and different. We have played the game before of who does he look like? Whose eyes has he got? Whose chin? As they grow up it is possible to see as well the way the boys' characters have similarities to those who have gone before.

On courses we do an exercise where we write on a flip chart words to describe God. Each time it is different but no matter what words are put up we share the characteristics of at least 80% of them because we have the likeness of God within us and so we have the capacity to reflect who He is. He is excited about us. Look at the picture of the way God created us :

> *The Lord God formed the man from the dust of the ground and breathed into his nostrils the breath of life, and the man became a living being. Genesis 2:7*

What a wonderful picture of active creation, an involved God moulding Adam with His own hands and then the Father stooping down to earth, and breathing His own life into His child. Those are not the actions of a disinterested, distant God.

WHAT IS YOUR IMAGE OF GOD?
God is revealed to us by:
> **His creation,**
> **by His Word,**
> **and by His Son.**

Do you know Him?
Unless we study the Bible for ourselves and form a true image of God, often what we believe about Him is based on our own story. Our perceptions may be warped by :

> - *the emotional wounds we may have received*
> - *the circumstances of our life*
> - *the relationship we had with our own father*
> - *our perception of authority*
> - *the teachings we have received.*

Generally, the world's view of God is that:
> - *He is not good*
> - *He is not in control*
> - *He is limited*
> - *He is made in man's image*
> - *and that I am God not He!*

We put God in a box.
> Have you seen the DVDs *'Indescribable'* and *'How Great Thou Art'* from Louis Gigilo? If your image of God means that He is manageable ... these will dispel the error! Looking at NASA's picture of the day or the Hubble web site has the same effect!

God is saying, "Know me" and you will know who you are:
- *A spiritual being*
- *Made to reflect the image of your Father*
- *Created for relationship with Him and each other*
- *Called for a purpose, to fulfil a unique part in God's story.*

The starting point for a disciple is to learn who God really is, the might and majesty and mystery but also the God who desires intimacy.

HOW DO I DO THAT?
RECTIFY MY IMAGE OF GOD

It helps to review the reality of what you actually believe right now. Don't go for the PC answer but look inside your inner world and discover what you hold there. These questions might help you capture the image.
- How did you picture God when you were a child?
- How do you picture Him now?
- Often we project the characteristics of the big people in our life when we were little onto God. eg if Dad was distant we believe God is distant.
- How have you experienced God in your life?
- What do you believe has been revealed of His character through your experience?
- Is this what the Bible says?
- Ask the Holy Spirit to reveal where you are mistaken and to rectify your image of God.
- What is God saying to you now?

Do record your responses: you will find it invaluable as this is not only crucial to your journey but will be the basis for an ever expanding relationship.

THE TRINITY

For me coming to an understanding of the different roles of the Father, the Son and the Holy Spirit was indispensable to my journey. However, it has also needed the exploration that comes with travelling together to get to know my God, person to person.

Though the three persons of the Trinity were united in their plan for the world, and subsequently for the rescue of their family, they have different functions within it. The role of the Father is the key.

The Fall meant that Adam and Eve could not be in the Father's holy presence. The Father's relationship with His children was unique and crucial, to flourish they must be in His presence. To restore family members and to bring them home the Father sent His most precious Son, the sacrifice that had to be paid for sin.

JESUS AND THE CROSS

 Of the three persons of the Trinity I had most difficulty relating to Jesus because my past experiences meant I did not trust men. So understanding about Jesus evolved slowly. I can remember in the early days being very angry with Jesus as I felt that He had only had a few hours on the Cross and I felt I had had a lifetime. I still can see and hear the horrified reaction to my speaking out such a thought in a housegroup.

My life in the church nearly stopped there. It was devastating to be condemned for such feelings and in my confusion and shame I shut down and wanted to run. We cannot choose our feelings. One reason Alpha has been so significant is that it lets people start from where they are, not where others think they should be. In his wisdom my pastor was not fazed by this 'outrage' but encouraged me to explore and seek what God was saying.

When you start out your ignorance is total and you do not know what you do not know. My pastor gave me *Derek Prince's The Divine Exchange* to read and a new pathway in the Waterfall Journey opened up. Suddenly, I saw the extent of what I did not know!

"Jesus was punished that I might be forgiven.
Jesus was wounded that I might be healed.
Jesus was made sin with my sinfulness that I might be made righteous with His righteousness.
Jesus died my death that I might live His life.
Jesus endured my poverty that I might share His abundance.
Jesus bore my shame that I might share His glory.
Jesus endured my rejection that I might have His acceptance with the Father.
Jesus was made a curse that I might enter His blessing."

"All your need covers every area of your life – your body, your soul, your mind, your emotions, as well as your financial and material needs. Nothing is either so large or so small that it is excluded from God's provision. By a single sovereign act, God brought together all the need and all the suffering of humanity in one climactic moment of time."
Derek Prince

That brought me to my knees asking forgiveness for my anger and blindness. Jesus paid the price for my sin that I might be free to live in the abundance of the Waterfall in the Father's presence. I wanted to embrace everything that the Father offered me in Jesus, to go beyond the cross and the tomb into the resurrection life. My journey to certainties has been slow and full of diversions and obstacles in which I have been grateful for the Holy Spirit's leading and guidance.

Learning about Jesus and entering into a deep relationship with Him is for all of us a distinctive, life time journey. As I have worked with people who are hurting I have observed some things that can block the way e.g.

not believing that He can do what He says he can

stopping at the Cross

not forgiving others

seeing my own sin as being too bad to be forgiven

Jesus served the Father and the family. He gave up His divinity to come as one of the lowliest on earth to recover the lost children whilst giving us an example of how to live as a child of God amidst the sin of the world. His life on earth, the Cross and the empty tomb point us back to the Father. Jesus took our sin upon His shoulders and suffered death upon the Cross so we can be without blemish as we return to the Father. His work on earth done, Jesus now intercedes for us before the throne of His Father.

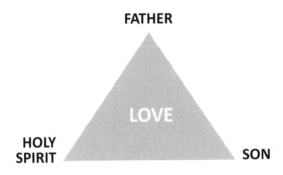

His going allowed the Holy Spirit to come to us. Now in the flow and power of the Holy Spirit, God's children, restored in relationship to the Father, can journey to wholeness and holiness being light in the darkness and being 'Jesus' in the fallen world. The Holy Spirit enlightens us and empowers us, revealing more and more of God's purposes and transforming us into the likeness of Christ.

These are good words but as ever the Waterfall Journey is about a living relationship. So many milestones are planted where I suddenly understood more about the persons of the Godhead, which brought a new facet of that relationship into a new reality with colourful living energy. It is a continual process.

....

Even as I am writing this book my inner spiritual landscape is changing and growing. Actually, this year has been pretty hard for many reasons and my continuing Waterfall Journey has been characterised by lurches as the ground has heaved, plummeting me into free fall and bouncing me along with the vigour of a fairground castle. Pretty normal progress then for me!

I was on a retreat in October with some of my companions on the journey when God did two major things in me in rapid succession, both of them a complete surprise, the effect of which has transformed my relationship with the Father.

On this journey one thing I thought I had mastered was keeping 'God out of the Box' I believed the Father could call things "that are not as though they are." I thought we have a 'can do God'. I thought I understood that but then I discovered that part of me did not. Here was a slice of me where trusting the Father was dangerous.

I was staying with Stephen and Prudence before the retreat and was engrossed in matters on my computer as they watched a Sozo video about something they would share when we were away. The Sozo ministry is about inner healing and comes out of the Bethel Church in California which is led by Bill Johnson.

The voice was saying, "Can you see a wall inside you?" Immediately I saw a forty-five foot high and an eight foot thick medieval castle wall. It was grey and made of huge blocks of stone and I was behind it, defended but confined. On the other side was the Father. The voice invited the audience to take the wall down.

Well, I demolished the wall for I did not want any separation from the Father and I ran to Him. It was such a relief to be with Him, a coming home but I was astonished for, I had not known there was anything standing between us. Shutting my eyes now I can feel the strength of the feelings of being home and safe and the rightness of it and suddenly understanding that I had not been in the place I thought I occupied in relation to the Father.

In the Sozo teaching the Father is the source of our identity, is our protection and is our provision. If that was not modelled well to us from our earthly father, we have trouble in believing that our Heavenly Father can do it.

In the preceding few months there had been the escalation of a threat that had been present for several years to part of my family. With gritted teeth I had stood in the Waterfall and on the Word and trusted.

However, the Father showed me that in this slice of me I doubted whether, when it was something that really mattered, He would come through for me. The root was my own father leaving me in the hospital when I had fractured my skull, I was waiting for my Heavenly Father to do the same. The threat of being abandoned by my Heavenly Father was so great that it needed such a wall!

The voice invited us to forgive our earthly father and to give the Father something and receive a gift from Him in return. I willingly forgave my dad, he always did his best for me and I simply gave the Father me. He blew me away for He gave me His heart. It was one of those organic, light bulb moments when life flows into understanding. I am His flesh and blood; He will protect that which I love with a protection that flows from His heart's desire.

In that transaction a whole new phase of my relationship with the Father came to life but He was not finished.

On the Tuesday of our retreat, in our time of worship, Carrol suggested we wash one another's feet. My reaction was instant and violent. I was taking my socks off for no-one. Inside feelings of panic and rebellion were somersaulting around. So what was going on. I knew immediately God wanted to teach me a new thing because by the violence of my reaction He was getting my attention. Later on at great risk, because I wanted to be open to the Holy Spirit, I let Stephen wash my feet.

The panic was about being vulnerable and hating my body, the rebellion was about survival and anger with the world. All things I recognised from past healing but what was God showing me here?

By the following morning I understood this was about provision and who I am and I met with the Father again. I was wearing a white robe He had given me on another occasion and now as He gave me a lily I understood His heart's love of me. He was revealing a new vista of how He wants to Father me and more of the meaning that lies within that new horizon. I was barefoot and free to be more fully than before who He created me to be.

These things have completely transformed my relationship with the Father. He has exploded into a whole new dimension of life. My daughter sells Gruffalo facecloths which come in a small hard disc showing the face. Put them in water and they break out into a full sized face cloth with a vibrant picture of the whole creature on it. I have believed God means what He says, I have believed in Him but suddenly intimately He has drawn me close and I have experienced an explosion of understanding, of a new level of His caring and love. Suddenly every aspect of His character and presence has broken out with a new vibrancy.

In the past I have believed in His protection and provision but now the Father who will do this for me is wild and awesome, so much bigger and more powerful than I understood. Now I understand so much more this is driven by how much He loves me. Like Aslan He is not tame and I walk with Him.

Our retreats are very much led by the Holy Spirit. We go with the space and flexibility to respond to the agenda which flows from God. This year He had but one agenda for all of us and it was all about the Father and for each one of us to be drawn into a new and deeper place with Him.

The endless adventure of the Desert Christian

Not that they beggared be in mind or brutes
that they have chosen a dwelling place afar
in lonely places: but their eyes are turned
to the higher stars, the very deep of Truth.
Freedom they seek, an emptiness apart
from worthless hopes; din of market place
and all the noisy crowding up of things,
and whatever wars on the Divine,
at Christ's command and for His
        love they hate.
By faith and hope they follow after God
and know their quest shall not be desperate
if but the Present conquer not their souls
with hollow things; that which they
        see they spurn
that they may come at what they do not see,
their senses kindled like a torch that may
blaze through the secrets of eternity.
                Paulinus of Nola

CHAPTER 10

LEARNING TO BE A DISCIPLE

There were experiences along the way that helped mould my journey of
discipleship. The things, once learnt, became footholds to aid me as I groped
forward step by step on the path.

DISCIPLESHIP

*To be a DISCIPLE means to learn, travel and live with a teacher. It is more
than the acquiring of knowledge which is the lot of the apprentice; it is
entering into a lifestyle, which embodies the values, the mindset and the
rhythms of the master whilst journeying with Him.*

Jewish boys who did well at learning by heart The Torah, the first five books of the
Scriptures that were available in the time of Jesus, might be invited by the teacher,
the Rabbi, to become a disciple and to study in depth with him. However, it was
understood that by following a particular rabbi, the boy would aim to grow up to be
like him in more than knowledge and viewpoint. To follow a rabbi meant to aspire to
be him. Therefore, before the boy made a commitment to a particular rabbi he and
his parents would want to know who the master was, what his values and purposes
were and what his nature was like. So too, we need to understand the nature of our
God whom we would follow as disciples.

THE DEVIL
One of the first big changes to my thinking after I was saved was to upgrade the
devil from a pantomime baddie to a dangerous being. Thanks to the Holy Spirit and
with Phyll to answer my questions, I began to understand the full perspective of His
involvement in our lives.

The big picture we saw in GOD'S STORY and the devil's influence on our personal
lives we have already seen as we looked at THE WATERFALL in earlier chapters.
Now we are going to look at what it means to travel in the world where he has such
influence and despoiling plans.

As a new follower of Jesus, you are vulnerable to the devil because this is perhaps the best opportunity he has to knock you off track, whilst you are still weak in faith and seeking to understand the new spiritual landscape.

HOWEVER, Jesus has the victory NOW over the devil in every circumstance, so the good news is the only power the devil has over our lives is when we hand it to him. However, we are not immune and so there are things to learn about how God lets the devil have a say in our lives and how to win our way through to or stay in the place of victory.

Some things it has really helped me to know :-

- The devil is NOT omnipresent, he can only be in one place at a time; neither is he omniscient and he is certainly not omnipotent. BUT we do need to take him seriously.
- He cannot stand to be in the presence of Jesus and if you call on the name of our Saviour the devil WILL flee.
- The devil is rampant in the world now but we are not of the world. We are set apart for the purposes of God. If we see the devil in everything, we give him power in our lives. Our eyes should be on Jesus, who He is and what He accomplished.

God allowed the devil to tempt Jesus at the beginning of His ministry and to be used in growing Simon Peter.

> Simon, Simon, Satan has asked to sift all of you as wheat. But I have prayed for you, Simon, that your faith may not fail. And when you have turned back, strengthen your brothers. Luke 22:31–32

Winning through to a place of understanding of what your ministry is and building up your spiritual muscle through trials is what the journey is all about.

The armour of God in Ephesians 6 is essential equipment for the disciple.

I watched a talk by Joyce Meyer on the television in which she encouraged the audience to "throw rocks at the devil" for we are the victors through Jesus Christ. She was saying, "Do not listen to the devil's lies. Do not give him the space to get close and to whisper his poison in your ear. See him off!"

....

The first time the devil and his army came to my room I was petrified. I had only been a Christian for a few months and I was just finding my feet reframing old Anglican ideas. It was late and I was woken up by the noise and the curtains blowing. In my head I saw the hordes of evil and the devil at the head, even though I had my eyes screwed tight shut. They filled the room and fear overcame me and on this first occasion I cannot remember why they left.

Fortunately I had Phyll, my prayer warrior friend to talk to and with her wisdom plus her confidence in the power of the name of Jesus I was encouraged, for I was both scared and worried about the experience.

The second time it happened was even more terrifying. The same hordes and commander but they were more intimidating: the noise, smoke and the colours were deeply disturbing. I knew I had to say aloud the name of Jesus but it was as though my throat were closed. I still had my eyes tightly shut but that did not stop me seeing the horrors. Eventually after a real struggle to form the words I managed to say the name of Jesus and immediately I was alone.

More talking it through with Phyll and I began to see that Jesus really was the victor. Phyll gave me the picture of my standing tall in the armour of God and pronouncing the name of Jesus with confidence.

So the third time it happened I was not terrified but ready. There was an escalation in horror again but I did not look upon that. Dressed in my armour I kept my eyes on Jesus and spoke out His name with ease. The devil and his minions fled.

This experience gave me a great deal of confidence. It does not matter if I am out of my depth; He is not. The Holy Spirit led me to the books of Rick Joyner, starting with 'The Final Quest' and 'The Call' which I found really insightful to my understanding of the battle we are engaged in.

Also I learnt that when a seemingly difficult thing happened, to look to God. Joseph sold by his brothers could look back on the lost years and see God's plans and purposes:

> *And now, do not be distressed and do not be angry with yourselves for selling me here, because it was to save lives that God sent me ahead of you.*
> Genesis 45:5

We were burgled one Tuesday afternoon. The back door was open but intact as the burglar had forced an entry through a side window. There was mess, where drawers had been opened and turned out but there was no disturbance in the atmosphere. I was touched by a peace.

It was housegroup night and I had felt for the first time that God had given me something specific and important to share. It was about five o'clock when I called the police. They noted the crime but were not sure when anyone would get to me. The meeting looked as though it would be a non-starter.

I looked around. We had little worth stealing except for three rings; one had belonged to my grandmother, a beautiful opal ring which had fiery depths. The family had bought it for her Golden Wedding present because she had always wanted an opal in her engagement ring but in those days it was considered to be an unlucky stone. I remembered her delight when she had received it.

The rings were gone. I can remember the sense of loss but also thinking whilst I waited for the police, "How are you going to turn this to good, Lord?" believing that He would.

After only an hour a policeman arrived who turned out to be a Christian. He completed the paperwork and investigation in good time. Fingerprinting would be done the next day. Recovery of the rings would be highly unlikely in his opinion, which proved to be correct.

I got to the evening meeting and shared what was on my heart, surprised at its power. The insurance money bought a kiln which was significant in the recovery of my daughter from a long-term illness. Amongst other things she made beautiful jewellery. Looking back there was no way that we could have afforded the kiln without the proceeds of that robbery. What a mysterious God.

Now one of my most frequent questions to God is, "What is going on here? What do you see?" No matter what the circumstances look like to us, if we try to see God's perspective and trust He can bring it round for good. We are not of this world and this was one of the first occasions when I was really conscious of God's peace throughout as He worked out His plans. It was God's opportunity to bring blessing and healing.

Things that others have labelled as the work of the devil have been God's way of strengthening my faith, my beliefs and my spiritual muscle as I have learnt to look to Him first. If this sounds a bit pious let me assure you that there is an ongoing situation in my life over which I have no control and means there is real danger for some of my family. There are devilish aspects but I stand on God's Word and victory which I have known along the way. I do not understand much about the situation but I know a Man who does. When my tummy churns and I am on the edge, I hold to the character and purposes of God and look to Him and with my eyes on the face of Jesus there is peace. Without Him I would be a panicking wreck.

Much later in my walk I was feeling really ground down and overwhelmed by life. The picture that came into my head was of standing sentry duty on guard with my back to a hill. Behind was in darkness and across the flat floor of a valley there was a tumultuous, squirming throng of the devil and evil. I was frightened, exhausted and slumping at my post. I felt isolated and threatened. There did not seem to be another living soul around.

Then there was a glow of light to my right which grew and grew until the whole of the hill except where I was blazed with light and, mounted on a horse, Jesus came into view. He stopped and dismounted and He came and stood with me and I felt energy and hope surge through me; I straightened and could stand my ground. Light was now flowing from Jesus to me and I too began to radiate light. I realised I could see many more people standing and radiating the light where Jesus had passed.

Jesus mounted His horse again but leant down and offered me His hand. I took it and was pulled up in front of Him, high in the saddle; from there the threat of the evil forces became smaller and I could see them cowering as the light of Jesus flooded the plain. My perspective changed as I sat before Him and saw what Jesus saw. Something organic happened within that experience and often I sit up before Jesus on that horse. I can lean back into Him and face what is in front of me, however threatening.

Jesus lifted me down and I resumed my place but now I was ready, alert and confident ; knowing I was not alone but connected by light to others and under the command of the High King. As Jesus continued round the hill, the light spread with Him and I could see thousands standing ready, waiting.

SEEK YE FIRST THE KINGDOM OF HEAVEN

1. OBEY John 15:14
You are my friends when you do the things I command you.

2. LOVE John 15:12
My command is this: Love one another the way I loved you.

3. JUSTICE Prov 21:3
To do what is right and just is more acceptable to the Lord than sacrifice.

4. PEACE Psalm 34:14
Turn from evil and do good; Seek peace and pursue it.

5. HOLY LIVING 1 Peter 1:15
But just as He who called you is holy so be holy in all you do.

6. INTEGRITY Matthew 5:37
Simply let your yes be yes and your no to be no.

7. GENEROSITY Matthew 5:16
Keep open house; be generous with your lives. By opening up to others you'll prompt people to open up with God, generous Father in heaven.

8. SPIRITUAL WHOLENESS Matthew 5
You're blessed when you get your inner world - your mind and heart - put right. Then you can see God in the outside world.

9. BIBLICAL KNOWLEDGE Matthew 22:29
You are in error because you do not know the Scriptures or the power of God.

10. FAITH IN GOD Matthew 17:20
If you have faith as small as a mustard seed you can say to this mountain, move - nothing would be impossible.

11. BLESSING PEOPLE
Jesus not only taught this but His constant healing of, training + serving others demonstrated how to do it.

12. DISCIPLE MAKING Matthew 28:19
Therefore, go and make disciples of all the Nations

That experience was very real for me and when I feel threatened being up before Jesus in the saddle I am emboldened. When I am weary, just leaning back into Him imagining Him taking the reins and asking Him about how He views what lies ahead helps me reframe my life into His story.

If you have read *"The Final Quest" by Rick Joyner* he describes these scenes and I am sure my spiritual imagination was fired by his book. However, the experience I have described was a real encounter with Jesus and has been significant in my walk.

In my ministry working with individuals I have seen the Holy Spirit quietly dismantle, in a host of creative ways, strongholds that have stifled Kingdom living. We all have these areas within us for we have lived in enemy territory. Claiming back the land that the devil has taken is why dealing with our pain and buried issues is so key for the disciple.

In these ways I have been fortunate to see God at work in my life rather than thinking that the devil was in charge of the activities or circumstances that seemed to be working against me. This orientation of my thinking was greatly helped by Phyll's training as she constantly urged me from the beginning to actively, *"Seek the Lord"* in all things.

David gave the same, the best advice he had to his son Solomon:

> *Acknowledge the God of your father, and serve him with wholehearted devotion and with a willing mind, for the Lord searches every heart and understands every motive behind the thoughts. If you seek him, he will be found by you. 1 Chronicles 28:9*

Jesus promised that as we seek we will find:

> *Ask and it will be given to you; seek and you will find; knock and the door will be opened to you. For everyone who asks receives; he who seeks finds; and to him who knocks the door will be opened. Matthew 7:7-8*

God is interested in growing our character and that takes time. At twelve years old Jesus had the knowledge to astound the learned men in the temple. Then we hear nothing of Him until he is thirty but we know that in the interim:

> *And Jesus grew in wisdom and stature, and in favour with God and man. Luke 2 : 52*

Even Jesus needed time to grow into the rounded wholeness that is maturity. There are many elements to growing if we are to be disciples of balance and wholeness. God will take the time to get us to where He wants us to be.

WORSHIP

My neighbours Christine and Raymond went to a church in the next village and had on more than one occasion invited me to go with them. It seemed natural after I was saved to do just that. For me church was a very special experience even though as a new Christian as soon as I heard any worship I began crying. Now I know this is one of the ways that the Holy Spirit begins breaking down the internal barriers within us.

Tears are good. I learnt to always go to church with a pocket full of paper hankies. Churches should be festooned with them!

I found worship mysterious and somewhat scary in the beginning and it proved to be another area where I needed to be open to learn what was happening.

I began noticing that in the worship some people seemed to be going to a place I could not reach. It was a mystery to me but I so wanted to go to that place too. I noticed the choice of songs and choruses mattered, that something that seemed to be building could be squashed by the wrong choice of a song or a prayer. Certain people did not seem aware of what was happening and could kill the flow but that as things got deeper the pace would slow and utterances and prophecies might come. What was going on?

To join in I needed to see what was happening. I appreciate that every worship leader reading this will be shouting out the answers. However, I have never heard what I am sharing explained to the people in the pews and when I got the picture of what was going on it was one of the most important light bulb moments for me because it opened up a pathway to the throne that I could travel.

My friend Phyll explained what I was missing. In worship there were different stages:

Firstly, there was the gathering of the people, with praise songs that brought unity and awareness of who God is to the hearts of those entering into the house of God.

Secondly, there was a quieter sequence with more reflective songs focussing us towards our Holy God. There are songs and hymns which 'carry the Spirit' and change the atmosphere, moving the worship onward.

Then thirdly, a moving into the Most Holy Place of the Father's presence where in awe and reverence, those leading and the congregation follow the Holy Spirit. Phyll likened it to moving through the Tabernacle built by the Israelites to God's design after the Exodus. It travelled with them through the desert and was the place where God dwelt amongst His people. Entry was firstly through the gates of praise in the outer courts, a place of sacrifice where people would gather; then moving into the Holy Place surrounded by the altar of incense, the lamp stand and the table of shewbread where once only priests could minister. Then onward into the Most Holy Place, the place of intimacy and holiness into the very presence of God. This, where the High Priest alone could go and that once a year, had been opened up for us by the death of Jesus when the veil, the curtain of the temple was torn in two.

I read the Old Testament passages in Exodus 35 – 40 about the construction of the tabernacle. Moses was given the details directly by God and in the desert from what they had and with the skills they possessed, the people constructed the tabernacle, that travelled with them and was the dwelling place for the glory of God in their midst:

THE TABERNACLE OF THE LORD

REPLICATES TRIUNE NATURE OF GOD + MAN

OUTER COURT - BODY - NATURAL LIGHT SUN + MOON
HOLY PLACE - SOUL - LIGHT FROM GOLDEN LAMPSTAND
MOST HOLY PLACE - SPIRIT - LIGHT OF GODS PRESENCE

THREE ENTRANCES - JESUS IN 3 ASPECTS

I AM THE WAY, THE TRUTH AND THE LIFE. NO-ONE COMES TO THE FATHER EXCEPT THROUGH ME. JOHN 14:6

ENTRANCE TO THE OUTER COURT

4 POSTS = 4 GOSPELS
4 CHERUBIMS FROM EZEKIEL. 15
LION - MATTHEW - KINGSHIP OF CHRIST
OX - MARK - SERVANT
MAN - LUKE - SON OF MAN
EAGLE - JOHN - SON OF GOD

HISTORICAL REVELATION OF CHRIST'S DAYS ON EARTH LEARNED THROUGH NATURAL MEANS.

ENTRANCE TO THE HOLY PLACE

5 PILLARS REVEALED BY THE HOLY SPIRIT THROUGH THE 5 MINISTRIES OF
EPHESIANS 4:8+11
APOSTLE
TEACHER
SHEPHERD
EVANGELIST
PROPHET
TO MAKE US WHAT WE SHOULD BE + TO BECOME MATURE ATTAINING THE FULLNESS OF CHRIST.

THE WAY

THE TRUTH

THE LIFE

OUTER COURT
HOLY PLACE
MOST HOLY PLACE

7 ITEMS OF FURNITURE
ALTAR OF BURNT OFFERING (SACRIFICE)
LAVER OF BRASS
ALTAR OF INCENSE (PRAYER)
TABLE FOR BREAD OF THE PRESENCE
GOLDEN LAMPSTAND
ARK OF THE COVENANT
MERCY SEAT - WHERE THE BLOOD OF SACRIFICE WAS FINALLY SPRINKLED. THUS MAN COMES TO HIS GOD.

ENTRANCE TO THE MOST HOLY PLACE - 4 PILLARS

JESUS THE LIFE IN DEATH RENT THE VEIL THAT WE MIGHT ENTER THE PRESENCE OF THE FATHER
HEBREWS 10 20+19
MATTHEW 27 50+51

4 PILLARS REPRESENT CHRIST'S WISDOM
RIGHTEOUSNESS
HOLINESS
REDEMPTION
1 COR. 1:30

THE MOST HOLY PLACE IS THE CONSUMMATION OF SPIRITUAL PROGRESS - WE CAN SHARE CHRIST'S MINISTRIES THERE OF PRIEST + KING HEB. 6:19 - 7:2

*Then the cloud covered the tent of meeting, and the glory of the Lord filled
the tabernacle. Moses could not enter the tent of meeting because the cloud
had settled on it, and the glory of the Lord filled the tabernacle. In all the
travels of the Israelites, whenever the cloud lifted from above the tabernacle,
they would set out; but if the cloud did not lift, they did not set out. So the
cloud of the Lord was over the tabernacle by day, and fire was in the cloud by
night, in the sight of all the Israelites during all their travels.*
Exodus 40 : 34 - 38

*I listened to some audio tapes by Derek Prince that explained the significance of the
construction and the furniture of the tabernacle which helped me to see the inner
significance. I also started drawing cards to try and capture the learning for me.
These things made the tabernacle live in my mind and when I was in church I would
walk through it as the different stages of the worship unfolded. It involved me with a
wonderful connection that always makes worship special.*

**HOW DO I DO THAT ?
WORSHIP**

1.RECOGNISE YOU ARE BORN TO WORSHIP FOR ALL TIME – it
is about giving the best, the deepest, the highest of ourselves in
ways that will bless and delight God and fill us with His richness.

2.RECOGNISE THAT ALL OF YOUR LIFE IS AN ACT OF WORSHIP

**3. WORSHIP IS YOUR ACTING OUT KINGDOM VALUES AS WELL
AS PASSIONATE CELEBRATION**

4. CORPORATE WORSHIP HAS AN UNFOLDING PATTERN – to
bring a congregation into the throne room, there are different
stages to be aware of and to be involved in.

5. BE AWARE OF YOUR RESPONSE TO WORSHIP – Different
personality types and the way your brain is wired can make a
difference to how you experience worship. You are very complex
and unique and for some it will be easy and for others it will be
more of a struggle to get through to the throne room. The way is
open for all of us but you may need to seek and discover how it
works for you.

For me it was the picture of the tabernacle , for some it will simply
be the music, for others it may be dance, words or silence. My

experience was that once I had found a way in, I discovered many more routes. There are ways to discover what might help you e.g. an Enneagram or an MBTI course looking at personality types and worship, can transform your understanding of how to enjoy worship on a new level. Talking to trained worship leaders or going on one of their training courses gives you the inside line.

6. BE OPEN TO NEW EXPERIENCES – On a recent course a friend turned up with some worship flags. I said, "You won't catch me jumping about with those!" I should have learnt by now! When we were worshipping, Jesus said very clearly to me, "Right now for the flags." Sheepishly, I went and chose a purple flag and began to waft it about self-consciously and then Jesus came too. The next few minutes I shared something with Jesus amongst the stars that I will never forget. Purple became significant, movement became significant in undreamt of ways. I learnt my lesson I will not say 'never' again, I might miss a deep joy.

7. THE THRONE ROOM IS THE START OF AN EXPLOSION OF WAYS TO WORSHIP FOR EACH ONE OF US. IT IS A GLIMPSE INTO ETERNITY – The throne room in the Father's presence is just the start. There is a wonderful chorus which points the way ;-
"Take me deep,deep, deeper into you
Lord I want to know you much more than I do
Take me higher until my spirit soars
Nearer to you Lord until I am only yours."

8. DON'T GIVE UP – how you experience worship is not a competition or a measurement of spirituality. We are born to worship so it is about finding your way. It is another of the 'Seek and I will be found by you' scenarios. As ever the journey is equipping you to help others who are struggling along the same path behind you .

9. WORSHIP IS NOT JUST ABOUT WHAT HAPPENS ON THE PLATFORM SO SHARE YOUR KNOWLEDGE AND EXPERIENCES – the highs and the lows. Then we can together in a richer encounter bring pleasure and blessing to our God.

WATER BAPTISM

I was quite put out when I was told now about a year into my walk that I should be baptised. I had been baptised when I was a baby so why did I need it again? This was not based on any theological objection but rather with the weight of life at the time, as my counselling was beginning to hit deep stuff and life itself was full of difficulty.

However, when it was explained to me, I experienced the coming alive in the heart which told me it was right for me. I was already experiencing the pull of His calling

Therefore go and make disciples of all nations, baptising them in the name of the Father and the Son and of the Holy Spirit. Matthew 28:19

And I did not believe you could take others where you would not go. I also wanted the going down in sin and coming up into life that would identify me with Christ's death, burial and resurrection and I so wanted to be clean. Romans 6:4.

I think in my head there were very simple pictures of what it meant, together with the compulsion that I wanted to obey and follow, therefore, I made the decision to be baptised. The event was very special, not least because my son and daughter came and my testimony felt like a watershed, a declaration that henceforth I wanted to live my life a different way, Christ's way. In the years that followed I gradually learnt more and more of the spiritual significance of that day. It was certainly a milestone for me and a treasured gift.

BAPTISM OF THE HOLY SPIRIT

 To begin with I did not realise that the baptism of the Holy Spirit was a contentious issue. What I had observed as I said above was that some people seemed to go in worship where I could not go and that often it was a prophecy or praying in tongues and its interpretation that did something to the atmosphere that took us to those deeper levels.

I was hungry for more of God. My reaction was forged in the years of darkness when I had locked God out of my life. Now in the light I was not going to shut any door He set before me. That hunger was a blessing because I wanted more of God not of religion. This was personal and nothing to do with doctrine. I have always been grateful for that hunger which has propelled me forward despite my fears and the infection of other people's misgivings. It has kept me moving.

What I share below is the way I experienced my introduction to the baptism, to tongues and the chapter it opened up for me in my story. If it sounds like an over simplification or naive it is because that is how I experienced it.

 *When people spoke or sang in tongues I was really freaked out to start with as I had no idea what was going on. Then I realised that there seemed to be a certain atmosphere present when it happened which would lead to the utterance or the singing but too much was going on for me personally to take much notice. I was still swathed in Kleenex for the entire service at this stage, crying incessantly.*

Then Roy our Pastor asked me if I would come to a meeting where his old pastor, down from Scotland, who had a ministry leading people into the Baptism of the Holy Spirit, would be speaking. As soon as he asked I knew inside me that I must go but I had fears, not made easier by the minefield of people's reactions to the very idea!

So I read what Jesus said. I read Acts and what Paul said about it and it sounded good to me. I accepted simply that having been saved there was a deposit of the Holy Spirit within me but to blossom the Baptism of the Holy Spirit was needed and that I would speak in tongues as a result.

Jesus said He had to go so the Holy Spirit could come. When He came it was with tongues of fire in the upper room and they all spoke in different languages, not their own tongues; as did the Gentile Cornelius and his household in Acts10. Jesus said, "Go and make disciples." How would we go with less than He gave to the Twelve? When Jesus was alive, the Spirit was with them on their training trips so they did miracles but this was something deeper and more significant.

> On the last and greatest day of the Feast, Jesus stood and said in a loud voice, "If anyone is thirsty, let him come to me and drink. Whoever believes in me, as the Scripture has said, streams of living water will flow from within him." By this he meant the Spirit, whom those who believed in him were later to receive. Up to that time the Spirit had not been given, since Jesus had not yet been glorified. John 7:37-39

I read the books 'Prison to Praise' and Jackie Pullinger's book 'Taming the Dragon', both of which are written to show the power of the ministry of the Holy Spirit.

The evening came and Roy and his wife took me and another man to the meeting. The whole adventure was a new experience with some two hundred people there with a purpose before God.

After a period of worship and the Word, explaining what it was all about the pastor called out those who wanted the baptism to the front whilst the rest continued to worship. I stayed in my seat. As I watched the Pastor go along the line, everything within me was saying, "No stay!" and my spirit was saying, "Yes go!" When he was about half way along I could not resist any longer, I went forward. When it was my turn the pastor told me to speak out praise of God, as I began to do so he tapped me on the shoulder and said, "Not in English!" and out of my mouth came words I did not recognise. I felt nothing.

Roy was beside me encouraging me as the pastor moved on. I just kept on letting words form and come though I felt embarrassed. The other man who had come with us did not leave his seat so journeying home I could not ask all the questions that were in my mind. What had happened? Had anything happened? I had felt nothing, so was it me?

Once home I lay in bed and spoke out words but it felt I was making them up.

At some point I said a word that sounded familiar, that made me think I was counterfeiting the whole thing and being disrespectful to the Holy Spirit to boot. It was a wretched night. Next morning I went round to Christine and told her I thought I was being irreverent. She said one of the ways she had got used to her tongue was to sing. So we started singing a chorus and then I let the words come as they would. When she said it was genuine I was very relieved but wisely she sent me off to Roy to talk through my fears. He reassured me and explained that with any new tongue you have to practise and suggested that I did it by the clock. So I started doing five minutes at a time and gradually I recognised the language building, sentences and cadences.

It all felt different the next Sunday when I could go deeper into worship than I had been before and a new landscape opened up.

In a church service not long afterwards, out of the blue as the worship deepened I knew I should speak out in my tongue. I would become familiar with the Holy Spirit's prompting but this first time I ignored the tingling down my neck and the compulsion to speak. The opportunity passed and I felt I had failed God for all time. In misery afterwards I spoke to Roy. He was all encouragement and so gave me the confidence the next time to speak out. One of my fears was that no-one would be able to interpret an utterance of mine but Roy was always there and did so, thus building my confidence that it was all of God.

Being able to speak in tongues has been vital for my ministry. As I have shared the Waterfall in many churches abroad the aftermath is that people come for prayer for huge things in their lives. Praying in tongues is praying God's best for them when I would have no idea where to start. Worshipping in tongues means that the Holy Spirit has a channel to take people where He wants to lead. It is all about Him.

Before the Fall our minds were designed to receive communication from our God, spirit to spirit. Since then our reasoning can shut us off from the anointing of God's revelation.

So why does speaking in tongues cause such division? Today not all people speak in tongues and those who do not can feel like second class citizens. Some find it difficult because the religious tradition they follow does not believe that tongues are for now; others lack encouraging teaching or the confidence to open their mouths and speak out seeming nonsense and for the left-hand brained amongst us our logic speaks against it.

Being in the flow of the Spirit in the Waterfall we can grow in many of the gifts of the Holy Spirit - prophecy, words of knowledge, wisdom, discernment, seeing pictures and visions - and yes speaking in tongues and interpretation. We need to be open to receiving any and all of these, confident that there are no second class citizens in the Kingdom of God and that in all these ways :-

This is what we speak, not in words taught by human wisdom but in words taught by the Spirit, expressing spiritual truths in spiritual words.
1 Corinthians 2:13

May I suggest that you let the Holy Spirit lead your teaching and equipping? That does not mean do not ask and seek but be content with what you are given and shown. God has His own timing.

Don't major on it as Phyll would say but be open and confident that as a disciple God will have gifts for you.

A GENTLE CHALLENGE
If any milestone is resonating with you, don't let the moment pass – explore and find out more. In your journey they can be real markers, signalling new landscapes ahead and new depths in relationship with your God.

NOTES

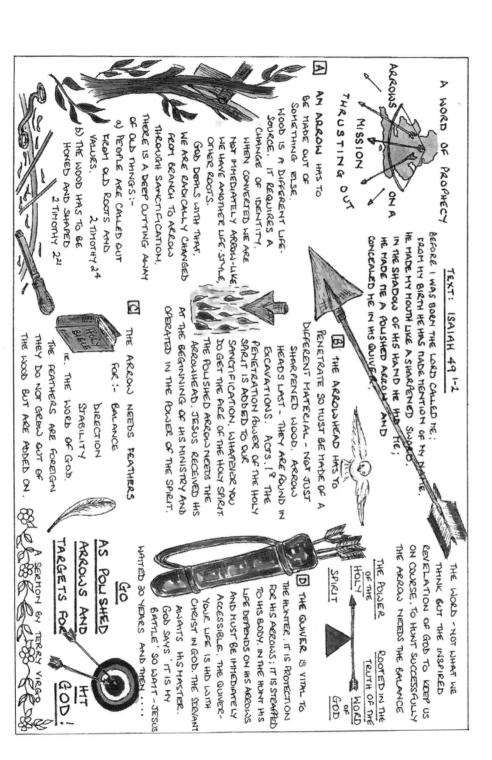

A WORD OF PROPHECY

MISSION THRUSTING OUT ARROWS ON A

TEXT: ISAIAH 49 1-2

BEFORE I WAS BORN THE LORD CALLED ME; FROM MY BIRTH HE HAS MADE MENTION OF MY NAME. HE MADE MY MOUTH LIKE A SHARPENED SWORD, IN THE SHADOW OF HIS HAND HE HID ME; HE MADE ME A POLISHED ARROW AND CONCEALED ME IN HIS QUIVER.

A AN ARROW HAS TO BE MADE OUT OF SOMETHING ELSE. WOOD IS A DIFFERENT SOURCE. IT REQUIRES A CHANGE OF IDENTITY. WHEN CONVERTED WE ARE NOT IMMEDIATELY ARROW-LIKE. WE HAVE ANOTHER LIFE-STYLE, OTHER ROOTS.

GOD DEALS WITH THAT. WE ARE RADICALLY CHANGED FROM BRANCH TO ARROW THROUGH SANCTIFICATION. THERE IS A DEEP CUTTING AWAY OF OLD THINGS:-

a) PEOPLE ARE CALLED OUT FROM OLD ROOTS AND VALUES. 2 TIMOTHY 2:4

b) THE WOOD HAS TO BE HONED AND SHAPED. 2 TIMOTHY 2:21

B THE ARROWHEAD HAS TO PENETRATE SO MUST BE MADE OF A DIFFERENT MATERIAL - NOT JUST SHARPENED WOOD. ARROW HEADS LAST - THEY ARE FOUND IN EXCAVATIONS. ACTS 1:8 THE PENETRATION POWER OF THE HOLY SPIRIT IS ADDED TO OUR SANCTIFICATION. WHATEVER YOU DO GET THE FIRE OF THE HOLY SPIRIT. THE POLISHED ARROW NEEDS THE ARROWHEAD. JESUS RECEIVED HIS AT THE BEGINNING OF HIS MINISTRY AND OPERATED IN THE POWER OF THE SPIRIT.

C THE ARROW NEEDS FEATHERS FOR :-
BALANCE
DIRECTION
STABILITY
IE. THE WORD OF GOD.

THE FEATHERS ARE FOREIGN THEY DO NOT GROW OUT OF THE WOOD BUT ARE ADDED ON.

THE WORD OF GOD - NOT WHAT WE THINK BUT THE INSPIRED REVELATION OF GOD TO KEEP US ON COURSE. TO HUNT SUCCESSFULLY THE ARROW NEEDS THE BALANCE

THE POWER OF THE HOLY SPIRIT
ROOTED IN THE TRUTH OF THE WORD OF GOD

D THE QUIVER IS VITAL TO THE HUNTER. IT IS PROTECTION FOR HIS ARROWS; IT IS STRAPPED TO HIS BODY. IN THE HUNT HIS LIFE DEPENDS ON HIS ARROWS AND MUST BE IMMEDIATELY ACCESSIBLE. THE QUIVER - YOUR LIFE IS HID WITH CHRIST IN GOD. THE SERVANT AWAITS HIS MASTER. GOD SAYS 'IT IS MY BATTLE' SO WAIT. JESUS WAITED 30 YEARS AND THEN....

GO AS POLISHED ARROWS AND HIT TARGETS FOR GOD!

A SERMON BY TERRY VIRGO

171

PART 5

THE REALITY OF JOURNEYING WITH JESUS

The next three chapters are about our response, the changes that happen in our lives as we begin to live life from God's perspective.

CHAPTER 11

THE SERMON ON THE MOUNT

To choose to live life in the Waterfall turns life upside down; there is a cost to discipleship. Kingdom rules, values and experience are often quite the opposite to 'ordinary human life.' We are called to be 'set apart' and it helps to think through some of the elements of life that will be changed if we are going to live in the will and purpose of God in His presence. Where else would you look but to the words of Jesus to see what that will look like?

One of the first cards I drew was of the Sermon on the Mount. It was a mind map of all the things Jesus shared at the start of His ministry that were key to people's understanding of the values of the new Kingdom. It was such a huge shift away from life lived in the fallen world but here Jesus was saying, *"Don't worry, look to me."* After years of trying to do it alone here at last was a different way. Here was Waterfall living changing the experience of day to day life.

HOW DO I DO THAT?
LIVE BY KINGDOM VALUES ON EARTH

1. READ MATTHEW 5 – 7 THROUGH SEVERAL TIMES
Jesus says in Matthew 7:24

> *Therefore, everyone who hears these words of mine and puts them into practice is like a wise man who built his house on the rock.*

There is so much meat in these chapters that it can seem indigestible. Where to start? So much to learn.

2. STUDY THE CONTENT

My response was to draw the card. It was my mind map so I could capture the breadth of what Jesus was saying to me in His Sermon. He starts with what makes us kingdom ambassadors both special and apart.

There were some new principles for me to take in. Jesus was saying:

- I am called to live righteously.
- How I deal with anger matters. It is my responsibility to take action but I also need to know God's wider perspectives.
- Not just my deeds but my thoughts need to be aligned with God's thinking.
- The way that giving, praying and fasting is done matters and as these actions flow out of my inner world the focus of my inner life is crucial.
- I need to have my eyes on the treasures of the Kingdom and reorientate life, trusting to God as my Provider.
- I have choices and I must take responsibility for them choosing not to judge, choosing to forgive freely, and choosing to follow closely on the narrow way.
- I need to be actively involved by asking and seeking, learning to recognise what is good by its fruit.

Keep re-reading the chapters Matthew 5-7 and use your own methods to keep before you these concepts so they began to be familiar to you. It is in these 'nitty gritty things' that we may be aligned to the Kingdom so that our everyday life will be salt and light.

3. CHANGE

So far these are the 'broad brush' concepts but where do you actually begin to make changes to your life? The good news is you sit back and relax and listen to what comes into your head and your heart.

- The Sermon on the Mount are the words of Jesus. Read them as though He were speaking to you face to face. Ask Him what He wants you to deal with first.
- Remember this is the work of the Holy Spirit.
- Follow and He will grow your faith area by area.

The way you are led will be unique to you.

4. SHARE
- Share what you are learning with someone who will encourage you.
- Share with someone you can encourage.
- Our testimonies have the power to build others up into Kingdom living.
- Be honest, be real. Telling of our mistakes and difficulties can bless others.
- As I was reading the Sermon on the Mount and asking what I needed to do, it became very clear where my starting point to change was to be centered. It leapt from the page to meet me. It was all about my attitude to money.

PROVISION AND FINANCE

Life in the Waterfall turns the rules of survival that many of us have existed by on their head as we come under Kingdom principles. One of the major changes for me was in this whole area of provision and finance.

If I look back on my life before Jesus saved me on that August evening in 1991 I see a battlefield in which I was trying to survive, where money was always an issue. It was exhausting trying to bring up children within two marriages where there was no support in either provision or in facing deficits, no sharing of values or action. I felt on my own as I tried to make life work.

My attitude to money could be summed up by 'Never go into debt'. I learnt this lesson at college, which reinforced the family value I had learned at home, that you do not buy anything if you have not the money to pay for it. This is great in theory but over the years living up to that, especially when it was about food shopping at the month's end, was a constant anxiety. It is safe to say I was neurotic about money as I stepped into the Waterfall.

Thus early teaching about tithing made my head ache. Ten percent! How was I going to do that? My husband was drinking away his pension and my two teenagers did not come cheap! However, I decided to obey because I wanted to do so, I wanted to be completely committed to Jesus, living life His way. From that day things began to change within me.

There were two early tests about money. In the first I went to the ATM machine knowing that the amount in my account was very low it being the last week of the month. To my astonishment there was £10026.00. I went into the bank and said there had been a mistake there was £10,000 too much in my account. The cashier asked me if I was sure! I was. They had shovelled someone else's money into my account but were very pleased to rectify their mistake.

The second incident happened when I felt prompted to stop to ask a Pakistani couple if they wanted some help. They were parked in a lay-by. The lady was pregnant and they were on their way to Brighton for a hospital appointment but had run out of petrol. I took the gentleman to a nearby petrol station and after he filled a can with fuel I drove him back to his wife. Then I said goodbye and drove off. I had gone about three miles when I looked down and saw his wallet on the floor. I raced back but they had gone. I looked in the wallet which was fat with cash, cards and a cheque book but no address. However, I was able to return it to the owner via his bank.

These two incidents I saw as my personal temptations set by the devil to try and knock me off course but as is so often the case he oversteps himself. He had chosen the right area of my vulnerability at that time but not in a way that had any chance of derailing me.

Following these two events I began to have some confidence that the days of screaming worry about money were past. I began to believe that God means what He says. He will provide clothes for my back and food for the table.

I was hopeless at buying clothes, the whole process was embarrassing and I hated going shopping (it was some years later that God healed the underlying wounds that fuelled this attitude). However Jesus says:

> And why do you worry about clothes? Look at how the lilies in the field grow. They don't work or make clothes for themselves. But I tell you that even Solomon with his riches was not dressed as beautifully as one of these flowers. God clothes the grass in the field, which is alive today but tomorrow is thrown into the fire. So you can be even more sure that God will clothe you. Don't have so little faith. Matthew 6:28–30

I began finding God knew better than I what I needed and where to get it, often at a discount. As I began to be aware of God's help I looked for it. If I needed something new I would ask Him. Then I would go to town and wander around until I felt to go into a particular shop. Usually I bought the first thing that I touched and it would be just what I wanted. When I needed smart suits for work, in a town I did not know on an impulse I went down a side street. There was a dress shop with a closing down sale. I bought three suits which I loved for less than the price of one.

I was really beginning to learn that God is my Provider, that which I need He will provide. It became an adventure trusting God for the money to live. Encouragement from Phyll was vital to me, keeping me on track. So I learnt that I'm not supposed to live like a pauper. If it is needful I asked and He gave. One day I was feeling pretty worn out and I said "Lord if I had £500 I would take Phyll and myself away for a week's break." Next morning in the post was a cheque from my Aunt for £500 so we went and were mightily blessed. Sometimes without much, God would ask me to give someone more than I had. I obeyed and we stopped running out of money at the end of the month and I learned to have faith.

Occasionally, God would ask me to do outrageous things like give my newly acquired computer to a pastor when I was in Uganda or give my last saved £200 to someone in need. He always blessed me and we did not go without. I began to see that it was God's way of shifting resources around the Kingdom.

However, I also found out that God made long term plans for my financial future too. In the early Seventies I took out an insurance policy that cost £5.75 a month *and paid up after forty years. Remember, this was during the years when I had banished God from my life. I had only been paying a short time when we moved from Northern Ireland to BAOR, where we were stationed with the British Army in Munster. There was a break of three years when I made no payments and lost contact with the insurance company. Then by a 'fluke' on a visit to Northern Ireland for a holiday and on going into the bank we had used there, I was given a letter from the Insurance Company that invited me to pay the arrears on the policy and to resume payments. It was so bizarre I still do not know how God organised that one! I did pay up and completed the payments. The policy matured the very week I needed THE EXACT AMOUNT to pay for a cabin in the garden to accommodate my son and his children. What a God!*

I know God will provide my family with all we need. There are frequent examples of His loving care in all manner of ways that make the verses in Matthew live.

I believe there is prosperity for each of us but it comes through learning the lessons He would teach us individually about how He will make us part of the Kingdom economy. I am privileged to have a friend who has significant financial gifting which underpins a strategic ministry for the Kingdom. He may deal in hundreds of thousands, to my hundreds, but the same principles apply. We need to be faithful in the small things and the larger will come but it will be scaled to our walk and purposes. What we can all believe in is that God is the God of abundance, He is the God of a measure pressed down and overflowing.

> *Give, and it will be given to you. A good measure, pressed down, shaken together and running over, will be poured into your lap. For with the measure you use, it will be measured to you. Luke 6 :38*

The Sermon on the Mount reveals the character of God and invites us to play a full part in the rule and reign of the Kingdom now.

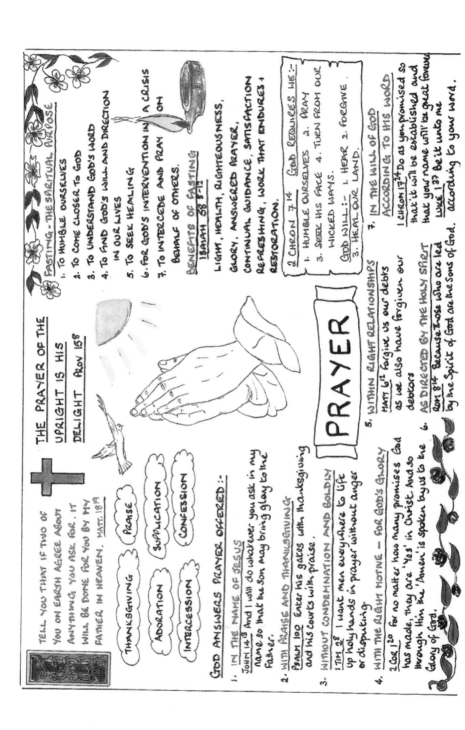

TELL YOU THAT IF TWO OF YOU ON EARTH AGREE ABOUT ANYTHING YOU ASK FOR, IT WILL BE DONE FOR YOU BY MY FATHER IN HEAVEN. MATT. 18:19

- THANKSGIVING
- PRAISE
- ADORATION
- SUPPLICATION
- CONFESSION
- INTERCESSION

GOD ANSWERS PRAYER OFFERED :-

1. **IN THE NAME OF JESUS**
JOHN 14:13 And I will do whatever you ask in my name so that the Son may bring glory to the Father.

2. **WITH PRAISE AND THANKSGIVING**
PSALM 100 Enter his gates with thanksgiving and his courts with praise.

3. **WITHOUT CONDEMNATION AND BOLDLY**
1 TIM 2:8 I want men everywhere to life up holy hands in prayer without anger or disputing.

4. **WITH THE RIGHT MOTIVE — FOR GOD'S GLORY**
2 COR 1:20 For no matter how many promises God has made, they are 'Yes' in Christ. And so through Him the 'Amen' is spoken by us to the Glory of God.

THE PRAYER OF THE UPRIGHT IS HIS DELIGHT PROV 15:8

FASTING - THE SPIRITUAL PURPOSE

1. TO HUMBLE OURSELVES
2. TO COME CLOSER TO GOD
3. TO UNDERSTAND GOD'S WORD
4. TO FIND GOD'S WILL AND DIRECTION IN OUR LIVES
5. TO SEEK HEALING
6. FOR GOD'S INTERVENTION IN A CRISIS
7. TO INTERCEDE AND PRAY ON BEHALF OF OTHERS.

BENEFITS OF FASTING
ISAIAH 58 1-12

LIGHT, HEALTH, RIGHTEOUSNESS, GLORY, ANSWERED PRAYER, CONTINUAL GUIDANCE, SATISFACTION REFRESHING, WORK THAT ENDURES + RESTORATION.

2 CHRON 7:14 GOD REQUIRES WE :-
1. HUMBLE OURSELVES   2. PRAY
3. SEEK HIS FACE 4. TURN FROM OUR WICKED WAYS.

GOD WILL :- 1. HEAR 2. FORGIVE
3. HEAL OUR LAND.

5. **WITHIN RIGHT RELATIONSHIPS**
MATT 6:12 Forgive us our debts as we also have forgiven our debtors

6. **AS DIRECTED BY THE HOLY SPIRIT**
ROM 8:14 Because those who are led by the Spirit of God are the sons of God.

7. **IN THE WILL OF GOD ACCORDING TO HIS WORD**
1 CHRON 17:24 Do as you promised so that it will be established and that your name will be great forever. LUKE 1:38 Be it unto me according to your word.

PRAYER

CHAPTER 12

YOUR TIME AT GOD'S DISPOSAL

Time is a funny thing – to our perception sometimes it seems to speed past and some times it seems to drag interminably; sometimes it seems to fill up like an expanding balloon and sometimes it seems to spill out into emptiness.

God is the master of time. Time is in His hands and time is rolling out as His purposes outwork. What does it mean to say all time belongs to Him?

To start with, God can alter time. He did so twice in the Old Testament.

 Joshua was marching out with his entire army to do battle with the combined armies of five Amorite kings. The Lord told Joshua not to be afraid for He was giving the enemy into his hands. He did just that, *"the Lord threw them into confusion"* after Joshua's force took them by surprise. Defeated they fled and *"the Lord hurled large hailstones down on them from the sky, and more of them died from the hailstones than were killed by the swords of the Israelites."* Joshua then prayed for the sun and moon to stop so that the Israelites might be avenged:

The sun stopped in the middle of the sky and delayed going down about a full day. There has never been a day like it before or since, a day when the Lord listened to a man. Surely the Lord was fighting for Israel! Joshua 10:14

The second time, a King of Israel, Hezekiah became ill and having prayed, God promised He would heal him. Moreover God would give him an extra fifteen years of life and He would defend Jerusalem against their enemies, the Assyrians. Hezekiah asked Isaiah, the prophet, what would be the sign that this would come into being:

Isaiah replied, "Shall the shadow go forward ten steps or shall it go back ten steps?" "It is a simple matter for the shadow to go forward ten steps," said Hezekiah. "Rather, have it go back ten steps." 2 Kings 20: 1–11

So how do you use your time? Most of us might feel that is a loaded question. Probably, what we would all agree on is that life is getting more and more frenetic and pressured so that maybe we feel that time rules us.

On the surface the pace of life seems to be ever speeding up. Stress and burn out are common with the constant level of communication facilitating the need to always be on the go and in touch. The family support system is more fractured and complicated by tensions of divorce and extended families. Now children are carers of adults, single parents run families, grandparents are looking after grandchildren and at the same time aged parents. The expectations of employers, spouses, children, schools, and churches, not to mention the State, are ever expanding. There is so much to do.

EXERCISE A:
SO WHAT DO YOU DO WITH YOUR TIME NOW?
This is a really useful thing to do and can deliver something of a surprise, for we can be unaware of how much things we do not really value can occupy our time!

DAYS	MON	TUES	WED	THUR	FRI	SAT	SUN

Make yourself a grid, spread sheet or list of how you spend your time for a week. Make as many rows as you need to understand your days.
- Do some thinking about what you have produced.
- Where do you spend the majority of your time? How do you feel about what you have discovered?
- What does your use of time deliver for you?
- What is the balance between work and play? Rest and activity? Your needs being met and the needs of others?
- What drains you and what replenishes you?
- Whose expectations are you fulfilling?
- How much of the time are you reacting to events and how much of your time is governed by your choice of activity?

To do this makes one aware that there is a bigger framework to the consideration of time than one week's activities. How does this week fit into the realisation of your life's hopes and dreams, into fulfilling your responsibilities, potential and desires, your God-given ministry?
Record your thoughts.

The logistics and expectations of just living today, the ordering of our lives is perhaps more complex and demanding than in previous generations. The truth is that we rarely stand back and assess what we are doing, so that our life is not powered by choice but driven by the necessities we perceive.

Often how we use our time is the way others define us and the way we judge ourselves. There is a tyranny to time that can control and deplete us.

Further, as we have seen earlier when we looked at the Problem of Pain, often when we are living our life with buried hurts, what we do with our time is designed to give us something to fulfil our needs. We may experience either a drivenness that fills our days or an emptiness that bleeds meaning away.

If I believe that to be of value I must have the latest phone, tablet, television and car, that status matters or that I must be seen to have a good job, those needs will set the parameters of how I spend my time. If I believe I must be in control to be safe, then I must manipulate people, circumstances and activities to deliver that for me.

Time can also seem punishing and accusatory e.g. if you have been made redundant or have M.E. or depression you or others may make judgements about how you are spending your time. You may experience time as empty and endless.

THE WATERFALL AND TIME

Time belongs to God. When you think about time from God's perspective the subject is massive. Time for each of us is finite and our life span is ordered by God :

All the days ordained for me were written in your book before one of them came to be. Psalm 139:16

God is very involved and an interested party in how we are investing our time. The potential and gifting He endowed us with also bears on how we make use of our time but it is bigger than that.

When I choose to live in the Waterfall, in God's will and purpose, I am saying in effect, "My time is yours." I am putting back in God's hands the gift He gave to me. Here in the Waterfall as I stand to live my life I am working for the Living God 24/7. The question I need to ask God is, "What do you want from me?" Discipleship means being available to God all the time, not just when we choose it or knowingly put ourselves at God's disposal but all of the time.

Getting time sorted out in my mind was a huge step forward in living in the Waterfall. In the early days I still saw life in compartments with God only concerned in part. When I reframed my life into God's story and the Waterfall I began to understand that God owned my time. It has been a journey of discovery to really see how that works. All the time I am in His presence I am available 24/7 for His service and His purposes.

Some of the time we work in co-operation by doing what He gives us daily to do, as part of living in the flow of the Holy Spirit, we deal with the logistics of life. Surprises and deviations, disasters and difficulties come with a reason. It is a good habit to enquire what God's reason might be. Sometimes we may not understand for some months; sometimes we never will. Often people will blame the devil for occurrences but it is God who is the Master. The devil will only be involved as God allows, as in the temptations of Jesus.

I was travelling home to my parents on one of my regular visits, when on an empty stretch of road I had a puncture. I patiently sat and waited for help, wondering why it had happened. For fifty minutes I waited for the RAC and then with the wheel changed I continued. Twenty minutes further on, at a bad intersection, there had been a crash. The air ambulance was just lifting off and cars were strewn across the road.

God said quite clearly, "I was keeping you safe." Now when I experience unforeseen obstacles to the 'smooth running' of my life, I ask God to show me what He sees. I know there will be some reason and sometimes He shows me what it is. What it does mean is that I am much more patient than I used to be, knowing "that all things work together for good" and that He is in charge.

THE EXAMPLE OF JESUS

How did Jesus spend His time? What were the principles that governed what He did? It starts right back with Jesus knowing who He was and that He had come to serve the purposes of the Father. The focus of His life was pleasing the Father by serving Him in the flow of the Spirit.

Expectations were heaped on Him from all quarters but He was not pulled by them to deviate from His Father's purpose. In each situation He would consider and respond to the circumstances and the needs of those involved according to the purposes of the Father. He never reacted in haste or out of need. In His wholeness He gives us the pattern to aspire to modelling how to balance this precious commodity that is time.

WHAT WERE THE BALANCES JESUS MODELLED?

The balance between activity and rest:

God was very clear about the ratio that is required of us. He rested on the seventh day and underlines our need for the Sabbath rest. The one in seven ratio for rest and refreshment used to define a working day, and a working week and at least schools still know the value for children that a rest one week in seven brings. Unremitting work and activity deny the design of our bodies to be restored and healed.

Over forty times in the Gospels Jesus withdraws to be replenished to come again. He did a range of things in those times but the activity He never compromised was time alone with His Father where at rest the peace and infilling that the world cannot know was to be found.

The balance between work and play:

Jesus would heal and preach while the Spirit was upon Him and then He would withdraw from the crowds. He would not allow Himself to pick up any responsibility that was not His. He did not do all the good things He might have done, He did the right things according to the anointing upon Him and the purposes of the Father.

As we follow in His footsteps in the Waterfall, in the flow of the Holy Spirit we too are being asked to do the things the Father gives us to do, not all the things that we might think are good. Excellent church and personal programmes, if not inspired by the Holy Spirit, are not helping God's kingdom plans. We all need to be doing the right thing from God's perspective not our own. If we are doing what God ordains we will not be overloaded with busyness.

Jesus had a loyal group of friends sharing travel and meals and purpose. They had time for learning, laughter, relationships and relaxation. These times together poured back in what had been drained out.

The balance between engaging and withdrawing:

There was a deeper level of replenishment required. The balance between expending energy, being drained and being renewed to come again would not have been possible without time alone with the Father, where Jesus was spiritually in-filled. This was the core, as the being of Jesus on every level was renewed through these intimate times with His Father.

Jesus was anointed for His ministry but He still had to be mindful of and manage the humanness of his energy flow. Jesus had both a self-awareness and a God-awareness. He was tuned to the flow of the Holy Spirit but He did not override the signals that His body gave Him. When He met the woman by the well in Samaria we see He too suffered from weariness. He was resting while the disciples had gone into the village to find food. It became clear that He was there for a God appointment and there in His physical 'weakness' was the anointing and strength for a very significant encounter. When the disciples returned and urged Him to eat He said:

> "I have food to eat that you know nothing about." Then his disciples said to each other, "Could someone have brought him food?"
> "My food," said Jesus, "is to do the will of him who sent me and to finish his work." John 4: 32-34

How differently we react, when "I must just…." often overrides our exhaustion time and again. Then in our busyness we switch off our tuning to God and self.

In this it is very helpful to know whether you are an extrovert or an introvert. This governs whether your refreshing is fuelled externally or internally .

My Mum was an extrovert. The grey days of winter and confinement by bad weather would drain out her energy and lower her spirits. When I used to visit my parents in Somerset I would get Mum out in the car every day and as we went along she would 'oooh' and 'aah' about things we would see, feeding off the colours and the antics of people. You could visibly see the energy flow back into her and enliven her whole being. Dad was an introvert; his renewal came from solitude and internal pondering and he would have been happy to spend the winter in his chair with a crossword puzzle and his paper.

Stress comes to an extrovert who does not have time to engage with others or to enjoy outside stimuli to colour their inner world. For an introvert stress comes through not having their quiet time and space to access their internal well of renewal. How each is replenished with God will be radically different and will govern how they experience and engage with God in their times of refreshment.

It is very also helpful to know where you are on your journey. Jesus, in the height of His ministry, was modelling these balances. As we mature and get older we need even more wisdom. The demand for engagement can be put upon us beyond our strength and outside our God-given ministry. How often do we do things because *'someone has to'*?

I have friends who were recently drawn by God to attend a new church. Immediately they were welcomed and invited to be on every rota and to join almost every activity the church offered. They are in their seventies and in the season of influencing not breaking ground, without maturity they would have exhausted themselves on good activities but not the right things.

A balance is brought through deep, grounding relationships:

We are born for relationship. Jesus spent time with His companions that was rich with engagement and revelation. He invested time in each of His disciples, in His family and in others who were part of His journey. Without investment, relationships wither and die for they are organic and need to be nurtured and fed and that investment will involve time. One of the joys of deep companionship where God is not just the invited third guest but the binding essence is that He is revealed and His mind is shared as we converse together.

The balance between pace and patience:

Jesus always had focus. From the beginning He knew where He was going, nothing diverted Him from the journey to Jerusalem but He did not rush the journey. He had a task on the way to train and prepare the disciples. He was endlessly patient with their obtuseness and questions and mistakes. He gave them time to learn. He understood the stages of the journey. There were times of getting the job done, times of travel, times of teaching and He understood how to lay foundations and let the seasons evolve.

I was working in the insurance industry and I was fed up. I so wanted to do more for the Lord so I prayed a prayer that I now recognise as dangerous! I asked the Lord, "Please will you get me to the place you want me as quickly as possible?"

Well, within a few months I had been made redundant but I created a business out of my insurance skills and had a successful year as a consultant to a London solicitors, teaching young solicitors what insurance companies needed from them to progress claims. Then there was a change in the law which meant the firm of solicitors replaced me with a much bigger organisation to do their training. However, now was my chance. I asked the Lord what to do and for the next six months I researched and produced and set up courses for vicars called 'Growth for God in the learning church.' At each stage I followed the directions of the Holy Spirit.

When I was ready and had the venues booked for six courses I sent out the invitations, over eight hundred across two dioceses. I got five replies and only two people wanted to come. It was a disaster. The courses were cancelled, I had used all my money, had no work and was given a dressing down by the manager of one of the retreat houses I had booked for the courses. He was scathing. I was not qualified, I had no degree, "Who did I think I was to run such courses?" was his theme and he did not hold back in expressing this.

I was crushed and angry with God. I had done nothing without checking with Him. I was also in difficulty about how to live and survive. I needed a job. I was stumped because my teaching diploma was deemed not good enough for teaching and I had no office skills so what was I fit for? I went egg packing, which may sound easy but we shifted sixty-five tons of eggs a week. It was hard work. After five long months I went to an employment fair to find work. There I got a job as a carer for a lady who had learning disabilities and challenging behaviours, who was being established in her own bungalow with twenty-four hour care after years of being in a mental hospital.

I worked with Emily for two years. In the first two months I was pretty proud of myself for doing 'a good thing' but as I began to get to know her, God was not impressed! He said to me, "This is not love. Love is taking off the rubber gloves in a bathroom emergency!" I learned that to care for Emily with love I needed to meet her where she was, to look at life her way and to work with her to recover her ability to make choices.

At the end of that time God brought together several strands of my experience to change the season. Having used the initial counselling training at CWR as part of my healing, He led me to continue training there in my spare time. Then God began opening opportunities for me to tutor on courses and to develop my own counselling practice that brought the prayer of four years previously to life.

Well, it was not the path I would have chosen. However, it was the pathway I needed to be prepared for my unique ministry, though it might look to an outsider as if it were a four year diversion. I learned so much on so many levels in those years, not only about God's provision and leading but about not making my own judgements and always seeking His perspective.

The Growth for God church courses would have been a success. It was the right stuff for the right people and I would have delivered it with panache but I would have thought I was God's gift to God. I would have taken the credit and I would have fed off it. God saved me from myself. Actually what I was good at under my control would have been lethal. This journey brought my gifting into the Waterfall and into the service and control of the One who knows how to use it and I am blessed.

God knew the way for me to travel, to learn from Him so that when He started putting back my ministry it would be God-centered and God-led. He took His time so I learnt at my pace. I recognise now how some lessons were repeated until I understood. Then it took a while for lessons to be consolidated into experience. There is time. Following Jesus in The Waterfall is about learning the lessons of pace and patience knowing the truth :

I will build you up again and you will be rebuilt. Jeremiah 31:4 :

He will do it in His time, the best way for both us and His purposes. God's roundabout route is the quickest and the best even though it feels like a roller-coaster in the backwoods!

EXERCISE B:
WHAT DOES GOD WANT YOU TO DO WITH YOUR TIME?

- Take a blank sheet of paper and begin with the question, "How does God want me to spend my time?" What do you need to include?
- What are your gifts?
  What is your calling ?
  Where is your passion?
  Do you know ?
  Where are you on the journey?
  Is God still training you or have you got to the place where you are operating in your full ministry?
- What about time for family and relationships, play, being, exercise and fun?
- Quiet times and fellowship?

Just stand back and invite God to help you write out how He would like you to be spending your time?

There is a very challenging truth that where we spend our time shows very clearly where our priorities are to be found.

This year for me has been 'The Year of The Book'. God made it clear that I was to write this book and that has been my focus.

It has been a journey of itself involving many stages of learning how to write, finding a discipline for working, deciding on the technology, finding my voice. The first four months were very up and down and haphazard as I strived to find my way and a rhythm of working.

However, there have been periods where the book has not featured. Between August and the beginning of October I was very clear that God wanted my focus on the family. Knowing that was the right thing I could put the book aside and give my full attention to where God was directing. This is so freeing, as you can relax into what God places before you, giving it your whole attention. Though I have my own deadline for finishing the book, it is not a legalistic burden but it is a helpful marker because I know I am working in God's rhythm and timescale.

EXERCISE C:
PLANNING CHANGES

You have discovered in the first exercise the way you are actually spending time and in the second where you want to be. When you have something on paper it will probably require some reflection time.

How are you going to achieve the changes you want? You may need a plan or your heightened awareness may help you make the adjustments you desire.

A great deal of the way we spend our disposable time is habit and changing habits requires us to take steps, and make an effort to break them, so some changes may not be instant.

If there are big changes you want to make break them down into stages. Also you may need to be aware how any change will impact those around you.

In Uganda I often stayed with a family in Kampala. My first night in Africa we had landed around 11pm – that drive home I will never forget. The darkness was alive with noise and bustle. The roadside was lined with people squatting around a few candles selling what they had, shops in shacks were open and throngs of people were shopping for the day's needs. Holding the images together in my mind was the smell of cooking meat. Africa seemed to be one big barbecue.

When we arrived at the family home we were met by Winston who loomed out of the darkness. He guarded the property dressed in a long coat, short wellington boots and brandishing a bow and arrow. Our faces must have been priceless.

I learned much from this family over the years. Every few months they would have a family meeting when each member spoke about how they were doing, their difficulties and triumphs and about how they were faring with other members of the family.

We had arrived after one family meeting where the youngest child of five had said to his Dad, "You're not my friend". The reason was Daddy was never home before bedtime during the week and often worked at the weekends. This statement was causing a radical rethink of the way the parents were using their time and had far reaching implications for the way they worked away from the home as well as refocussing time for the needs of each child.

There are seasons for the use of our time for Kingdom purposes:

- There are learning and growing years when the acquiring of knowledge and the development and practice of our gifting are the priority.

- Then there are the years of energy and action in the full flow of our ministry.

- Finally, the years of influence when the wisdom and experience passed onto the succeeding generation will create a Kingdom legacy.

There are also seasons to family life. God puts family before ministry on His priority list. We do not always do the same!

I am hugely privileged in travelling with a group of people who are deeply committed to Waterfall living. Most of us have travelled together over a number of years and are getting on a bit and are finding a change of season upon us, away from doing and towards influencing. We are spread over the country and though we have had diverse ministries we see some similarity in what God is leading us into now. The years of great energy have passed but vast reserves of wisdom and experience have been harvested by each one.

Now God is moving us all into places where we can influence and grow the succeeding generations and there is a picture emerging of a far-flung but connected network of elder statesmen and women of the Kingdom making themselves available, to mentor and grow the people of God. They are passing the baton onwards.

In such changes of season, strategic Kingdom thinking is needed by each individual. The whole of time has to be reframed to the new season but also all of us regularly need course adjustments to whatever season we are in.

HOW DO I DO THAT?
KNOW THAT MY TIME IS WITHIN GOD'S
WILL AND PURPOSE.

REVIEW YOUR USE OF TIME EVERY THREE MONTHS – What are you doing with your time right now? Sit down and do some big picture thinking of God's perspective on your use of time. Where do you want to be in a year? Five years ? Ten years? Brainstorm with God. Create a vision.

WHAT IS HIS FOCUS FOR YOU FOR THE NEXT THREE MONTHS? What amount of time will this occupy in your week? Think it through and picture what it will look like. Draw a plan of your week.

PUT IN YOUR BEING TIME Your quiet times and replenishing times should have high priority.

WHAT ARE THE RIGHT THINGS FOR YOU TO BE DOING? Bearing in mind the season you are in, your responsibilities, work, church and family commitments, how will you distribute your time? Think about the example of Jesus and apply those principles.

MAKE A REALISTIC PLAN. This should be seen as a helpful guide and not a legalistic burden but regularly review it.

NOTES

THE SEVEN MAJOR 'I AM'S' OF ST. JOHN'S GOSPEL

I AM THE BREAD OF LIFE. HE WHO COMES TO ME WILL NEVER GO HUNGRY AND HE WHO BELIEVES IN ME WILL NEVER BE THIRSTY. 6:35

I AM THE TRUE VINE AND MY FATHER IS THE GARDENER. HE CUTS OFF EVERY BRANCH IN ME THAT BEARS NO FRUIT. REMAIN IN ME AND I WILL REMAIN IN YOU. 15:1

I AM THE WAY AND THE TRUTH AND THE LIFE. NO-ONE COMES TO THE FATHER EXCEPT THROUGH ME. IF YOU REALLY KNEW ME YOU WOULD KNOW MY FATHER AS WELL. 14:16

I AM THE LIGHT OF THE WORLD. WHOEVER FOLLOWS ME WILL NEVER WALK IN DARKNESS BUT WILL HAVE THE LIGHT OF LIFE. 8:12

I AM THE RESURRECTION AND THE LIFE. HE WHO BELIEVES IN ME WILL LIVE EVEN THOUGH HE DIES AND WHOEVER LIVES AND BELIEVES IN ME WILL NEVER DIE. 11:25

I AM THE GATE FOR THE SHEEP; WHOEVER ENTERS THROUGH ME WILL BE SAVED.

I AM THE GOOD SHEPHERD. I KNOW MY SHEEP AND MY SHEEP KNOW ME —JUST AS THE FATHER KNOWS ME AND I KNOW THE FATHER — AND I LAY DOWN MY LIFE FOR THE SHEEP. 10:14

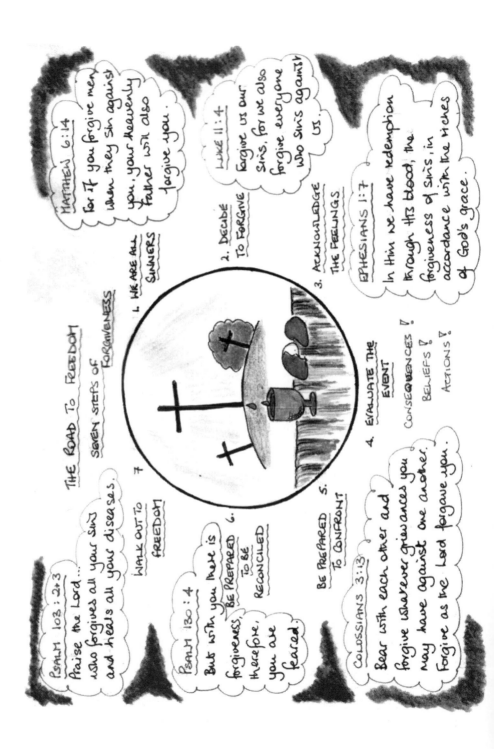

THE ROAD TO FREEDOM

SEVEN STEPS OF FORGIVENESS

MATTHEW 6:14

For if you forgive men when they sin against you, your heavenly Father will also forgive you.

1. WE ARE ALL SINNERS

LUKE 11:4

Forgive us our sins, for we also forgive everyone who sins against us.

2. DECIDE TO FORGIVE

3. ACKNOWLEDGE THE FEELINGS

EPHESIANS 1:7

In Him we have redemption through His blood, the forgiveness of sins, in accordance with the riches of God's grace.

4. EVALUATE THE EVENT

CONSEQUENCES?
BELIEFS?
ACTIONS?

PSALM 103:2+3

Praise the Lord... who forgives all your sins and heals all your diseases.

7 WALK OUT TO FREEDOM

PSALM 130:4

But with you there is forgiveness, therefore, you are feared.

6. BE PREPARED TO BE RECONCILED

5. BE PREPARED TO CONFRONT

COLOSSIANS 3:13

Bear with each other and forgive whatever grievances you may have against one another. Forgive as the Lord forgave you.

CHAPTER 13

SIN, FORGIVENESS AND FREEDOM

 Conflict is part of every life; it ripped its way into the fabric of our lives when man chose to disobey His Father and so disrupted the harmony of heaven's way. It is one of the devil's favourite weapons. When Jesus delivered The Sermon on the Mount (Matthew 5-7) we had God's own word on how we can rectify the damage and live righteous lives in His image and reflecting His glory.

Prior to His coming, sin had to be atoned for by sacrifice to appease the Law. Sin was an action that broke a written rule but in Matthew 5 Jesus is saying that our feelings, our anger can be wrong; our judgements, our thinking can be wrong; the way we do things, the choice of our behaviour, how we pray or fast can be wrong. He was saying it is what goes on inside us that causes us to sin. When Jesus died on the Cross for us He was the bridge for us to return into the presence of the Father because His blood paid the price for all sin. He was The Father's rescue plan for mankind.

Forgiveness flowing from the Cross is the greatest gift that Jesus gave us. It means we can be far from the finished article in the sanctification stakes but still because of Jesus we can stand in the Father's presence clothed in His righteousness, clean and upright because of His blood.

What is the key? To seek forgiveness and to be forgiven. That begs the question, *"Do I know when I have sinned?"*

Unfortunately, for whatever reason, sin and forgiveness are not taught about enough in churches today. It seems that many people, having asked for forgiveness when they come to Christ, feel they are then okay. There is a general concept that sin is only about big things like theft and murder. In the one-to-one work I have done over the years, in groups of seekers on courses and retreats, the lack of understanding of how full of sinful ways we are has been the most obvious deficit in knowledge I have come across.

Why was that so obvious to me? Only because I became aware of how full of sin I was but in the beginning I was blind to the planks in my eyes :

Why do you look at the speck of sawdust in your brother's eye and pay no attention to the plank in your own eye? Matthew 7: 3

In my healing journey the most painful part was finding out, oh so many times that what I thought was okay was actually sinful but I also learned why this was so. Being out of The Father's presence, outside the Waterfall, the lack of nourishment, the emptiness and the fallen world organically changes us. When we are back in the Waterfall we need a full overhaul, a look at our physical world and inner world, our thinking , feelings and our choices and our identity. At every point where what we do, think, say and believe is not aligned with God it is sin.

When I had an eating problem I knew it was pretty complicated and wrapped around my view of myself and clothes. Over the years I battled to keep my weight down. It was cyclical. Typically, I would screw myself up and battle to diet and do well if my mind was in the right place but struggle dismally if it was not. Hard won gains might be enjoyed for several months and then I would sabotage myself and eat more, knowing it was undoing the good work I had done.

About six years ago a book was recommended to me called, 'Love to eat hate to eat' by Elyse Fitzpatrick. As I sped through it, a page stood out which detailed exactly my story and from that page one sentence stood out declaring that my behaviour was sinful. Well I was a bit narked at that – for all of thirty seconds – and then it hit home. Oh joy, it was sin!

Why was I so happy? Because I knew what to do with sin. I knew how to work through to understand this piece of my story. I knew I could be forgiven and bring this segment of my being into the Waterfall. We have seen this process in Chapter 5: Understanding Ourselves. Healing was possible because this was the Holy Spirit's time to deal with this in me.

These two mind maps detail for me the journey the Holy Spirit took me on to unravel my eating story and to be able to see and recognise the precise nature of the sin that lay at the core, so that I might be forgiven, healed and restored in this area. Again I was amazed at how complex and far reaching was my woundedness. The unravelling came as I saw each element was sinful, so that bit by bit I could be forgiven and shift my position to a Godly place. It was such a huge relief to be free.

THE EATING SOLUTION I

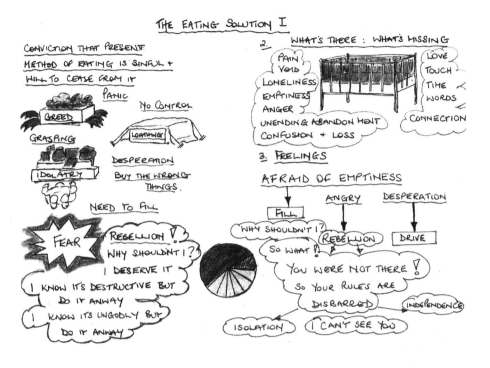

CONVICTION THAT PRESENT METHOD OF EATING IS SINFUL + WILL TO CEASE FROM IT

PANIC

GREED

GRASPING

IDOLATRY

No CONTROL

LOATHING

DESPERATION BUY THE WRONG THINGS.

NEED TO FILL

FEAR

REBELLION!
WHY SHOULDN'T I?
I DESERVE IT
I KNOW IT'S DESTRUCTIVE BUT DO IT ANYWAY
I KNOW ITS UNGODLY BUT DO IT ANYWAY

2. WHAT'S THERE : WHAT'S MISSING

PAIN
VOID
LONELINESS
EMPTINESS
ANGER
UNENDING ABANDONMENT
CONFUSION + LOSS

LOVE
TOUCH
TIME
WORDS
CONNECTION

3. FEELINGS

AFRAID OF EMPTINESS

FILL
WHY SHOULDN'T I?
So WHAT!?

ANGRY
REBELLION

DESPERATION
DRIVE

YOU WERE NOT THERE!
So YOUR RULES ARE DISBARRED

INDEPENDENCE

ISOLATION

I CAN'T SEE YOU

THE EATING SOLUTION II

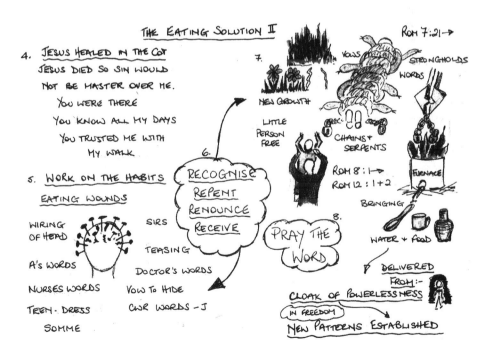

4. JESUS HEALED IN THE COT
JESUS DIED SO SIN WOULD NOT BE MASTER OVER ME.
YOU WERE THERE
YOU KNOW ALL MY DAYS
YOU TRUSTED ME WITH MY WALK

5. WORK ON THE HABITS
EATING WOUNDS

WIRING OF HEAD
A's WORDS
NURSES WORDS
TEEN. DRESS
SOMME

SIRS
TEASING
DOCTOR'S WORDS
VOW TO HIDE
CWR WORDS - J

6.
RECOGNISE
REPENT
RENOUNCE
RECEIVE

7.
NEW GROWTH
LITTLE PERSON FREE

VOWS
STRONGHOLDS
WORDS

CHAINS + SERPENTS

ROM 7:21→

ROM 8:1→
ROM 12:1+2

FURNACE

BRINGING

WATER + FOOD

8.
PRAY THE WORD

DELIVERED FROM:-
CLOAK OF POWERLESSNESS
IN FREEDOM
NEW PATTERNS ESTABLISHED

FORGIVING OTHERS

 What we often do not realise is that when anyone harms us, a giant hook is inserted into the flesh of our shoulders with a chain that links us back to the perpetrator. If we forgive the person, the hook comes out and the link is broken and we are free. However, in our unforgiveness many of us are bent double, dragging an O2 Arena full of people behind us.

The effect of unforgiveness is toxic as we carry it around in our lives. It ferments within us and anger at our treatment can turn into bitterness. The resentment can fuel a desire for revenge or just can snag us up so that we stay in victim mode. It can have physical repercussions on our health and can retard the work of the Holy Spirit within us. People change when they forgive. I have seen an ex-soldier who was perpetually bowed and shuffling, regain his military bearing when he forgave someone who had seriously harmed him. He said he could not believe how light he felt afterwards and a week later he was still flexing his shoulders in disbelief at the difference it made to him.

What did Jesus say? Well, He was uncompromising about two things - judgement and forgiveness. In 'The Lord's Prayer' Jesus says :

For if you forgive men when they sin against you, your heavenly Father will forgive you. But if you do not forgive men their sins your Father will not forgive your sins. Matt 6: 14 – 15

Repentance and forgiveness are the oil that smoothes the advance of the Kingdom. Jesus could abide in the Father's presence as He walked the earth because He was sinless and righteous. How different are we but when we repent and are forgiven we are washed clean and we too can abide in the Waterfall of God's love to live our lives.

Forgiveness is not easy. When the disciples asked how many times they were to forgive, Jesus said "Seventy times seven", in other words an unlimited number of times. I have always been so grateful for that. When I am getting things wrong time and time again there is no ticking clock. I have time to learn.

Forgiveness is a process which takes time.

We were born to live free of the burden of sin and unforgiveness, which squash the divine shape we were born to fill and would block us from the presence of the Father but for the sacrifice of Jesus. His blood is available to us that we might be washed and be clean and stand, clothed in His righteousness before the Father. The blood of Jesus sets us free as we seek forgiveness.

THE MIRACLE OF FORGIVENESS

The road to Gulu still felt spooky. The last 20 km of road was a single track red ribbon of dusty earth very often walled on each side with eight foot high, dense elephant grass. It was a tunnel made for snatchers where many had been taken in the years when The Lord's Army rebels had operated in this Northern region of Uganda. The dwellings, manyattas, came in large clusters where people gathered hoping the weight of numbers would keep them safe from slaughter, mutilation and kidnap.

The road to Gulu

The reign of terror which lasted years changed the landscape, it was too risky to be out working the land; there were killing fields, sites of horrendous massacres; children were taken; boys were forced to kill members of their own families and then join the fighters; girls and women were taken and abused.

In 2009 Pam and I and a team of four ladies led by Olivia, whom I had known and worked with annually since 2001, were travelling to Gulu, Kampala Pentecostal church's northern outpost. As well as a church, KPC had built a Watoto orphans' village and had established a working community called Living Hope for women who had been abused by the Lord's Army and needed to provide for themselves and the children that they returned with after the stolen years.

Olivia and her ladies were old friends of ours. The Waterfall had been God's instrument to change their lives and ministries and we all not only knew its power but in the intervening years had seen God spread the work. The Ugandans' appetite for a deeper and closer walk with the Father fuelled amazing ministries. Olivia and the other team members were key people caring for the children of Watoto with whom I had worked over a number of years. Already on this trip this team had shared special times together of work, revelation, worship and common purpose as Pam and I were also doing a lot of work with Watoto in Kampala.

Gulu was like a wild west town. It had not long been safe and one of the reasons we were here was to run a day for the Living Hope ladies, victims of the war who were trying to rebuild their lives.

The day dawned. As a team we had talked of what we would do. The first priority was The Waterfall and then we wanted to address their pain, so I put together a programme that looked good to us. As the ladies came in a heaviness came in too. Though they were wearing bright colours, their dark eyes and the weight of the past, bleached away any vibrancy from the scene. They put effort and themselves into the worship but it was rooted to the ground. Here Pam, Olivia and the team came into their own, spreading through the church they held us all through the singing and into the teaching.

As I shared the Waterfall story explaining that the identity of the ladies was what God said and not what the world said, we struggled. Some were trying to grasp hope, many were just blank but they had come believing God had something for them this day and they had a determination not to miss it. I knew very well by then to trust God to deliver through His truths, that all I needed was to deliver faithfully what He gave me. We talked of how problems develop and how seasons do change on our journey and that back in the Waterfall of God's love and presence healing and restoration were possible.

We talked of committing all now to God, in the Waterfall and that now a different, deeper relationship with the Father could develop. Often when people make the decision to live their life in the Waterfall they find it helpful to do something physically, so I drew an imaginary line and invited the ladies to cross it. We prayed and they all came out and over the line. We spent the morning exploring what life in the Waterfall would look like.

Yet at lunchtime I was overawed. I knew we had planned to deal with their pain but the weight of it, how could I lead it when I had no capacity to understand their experience? Olivia came up to me, "You are going to deal with their pain aren't you!" It was not a question. When I said maybe she should lead as the countrywoman of these ladies she said it was to be me.

We gathered the team and prayed and as we did so I felt God wanted the programme to be radically different to what I had planned. God has done this to me before and it gave us great confidence because I know then that the Holy Spirit will be in full flow so I just need to follow. All I had was how to begin. What God had shown me was to use the framework for dealing with abuse under four headings as you might do in counselling. The four areas deal with betrayal, trauma, guilt and powerlessness. I knew I had to start with betrayal but not how things would unfold. The whole team would hold us all in prayer and Pam and Olivia would feed insights to me as we went along.

The ladies had a special lunch and were gathered back together and there began the most extraordinary and literally awesome afternoon as we watched the Holy Spirit transform the lives of these ladies.

I started with what I had been given. Betrayal. I spoke simply of the way they had each been betrayed by the men who had abducted and abused them. Then I felt that they needed to know that this outrage made us angry, so I started voicing my anger for what they had gone through. The team joined in. We got quite noisy and then something broke and the ladies started joining, in letting go of their pain. It started slowly with odd words and shouts from them but soon the noise rose to a crescendo of shrieks, screams and rage.

After some time the noise abated and then I asked if they would forgive those who had so abused them. We talked about why forgiveness was important, a command from Jesus, a decision. What I was saying was being translated and one of the ladies spoke up and said she wanted to forgive. I suggested they spoke out their forgiveness and with tears torn from within and cries of anguish they spoke it out.

As they were doing so I noticed some men sitting outside the church. I went out to them and asked if they would come in and stand as representatives of the men of the Lord's Army and ask forgiveness of the ladies. They came, eight of them and stood in front of the sixty emotionally raw and volatile women.

For the next quarter of an hour it was a privilege to be in that place. I asked if one of the men could voice what a repentant leader of that army might say to ask forgiveness of these ladies. One of the men volunteered and he launched into a long speech in their language. I have no idea what he said except he spoke the words of God over those ladies. The effect was universal: the ladies started crying, a deep seated welling up and letting go. When he finished there was a completely different atmosphere in the room. The ladies looked emotionally exhausted but the heaviness had been broken and light was back in the room. I have always considered those men to be God's special provision for there was no reason at all for them to have been there at that time. Their courage, the power of the words they uttered and their effect could only have been inspired by the Holy Spirit.

We went straight onto laying down guilt and shame, speaking of the cleansing and forgiveness in the blood of Jesus. We buried them at the foot of the Cross and stood in the Waterfall letting the crystal river of love that flows from the throne of heaven flow over us and through us, washing away the stains and blemishes, leaving us pure and free, defined by who God says we are in Him.

The team during the afternoon were constantly alert, standing back, moving beside one and another of the ladies, holding out a hand as guided by the Holy Spirit. About this time in the afternoon, Olivia and Pam said that they both thought new names were going to be important. At the end of the day we were going to give each lady a card with the Waterfall teaching and a card from the nuns of a Carmelite Monastery in Norfolk. This card has a scripture verse on one side and a picture on the other. I give these cards out wherever I go as they are a direct message from the Father to the recipient and bring amazing blessings. So we decided that the team would also write a new name for each lady on the back of their card.

We continued by praying. I asked each lady to see Jesus standing in front of her and invited them to share what they wanted to say to Him and He would respond. I am always confident of saying that because Jesus will always act within His character. Conversations took place and then I asked the question Jesus often asked people. "What do you want?" More time elapsed and you could see work being done through the whole room. Then I felt to say, "Jesus now wants to bring you healing to your deepest wounds. Where is that for you? Now Jesus is reaching to touch and heal you and finally He wants to heal your broken heart. The heart of Jesus is next to your heart and life is pouring from His to yours; feel it beat strongly again."

Then I saw Jesus take each one of the ladies by the hand and lead them towards the throne room. I saw this like watching a film so I just relayed to them the pictures that came to me. First, they were dressed in new white dresses and as they entered they were given a royal cloak which Jesus draped over their shoulders; then they had to stoop and pick up their power as women of God before Jesus led them before the Father. There God said He would be the father and husband in their homes and mother and father to them. To signal the new place, each of them were to be given the new name by Him.

The team then moved amongst them and gave them their card with a message from the Father and their new name. Joy broke out. There was singing and laughing and praise and worship that lifted the roof off.

As a team we learnt so much that day but what stood out for all of us was that the day changed when those ladies took the decision to forgive. The ladies who went out had sparkling eyes and energy and colour.

NOTES

HOW DO I DO THAT ?
FORGIVE OTHERS
THE PROCESS – FIRSTLY ON YOUR OWN OR WITH
SOMEONE YOU TRUST:-

1. ACKNOWLEDGE we are all sinners.

We all start in the same place as sinners saved by grace and we have
seen that we all need forgiveness because we have picked up sinful
thinking, choices and behaviours living in the fallen world. No-one
is immune. Therefore, as we look on those who have harmed us it is
really helpful to remember those words of Jesus :

> *Do not judge, and you will not be judged. Do not condemn and*
> *you will not be condemned. Forgive, and you will be forgiven.*
> *Give, and it will be given to you. A good measure, pressed down,*
> *shaken together and running over, will be poured into your lap.*
> *For with the measure you use it will be measured to you. Luke*
> *6:37-38*

Frankly, we might feel nothing like complying at this stage but no
matter, just acknowledging we too are sinners is the start.

2. DECIDE TO FORGIVE – FORGIVENESS IS A DECISION NOT A FEELING

If we wait to feel okay about forgiving we may never do it. Once the
decision has been made, it allows God to work in us. It is a process in
which our feelings may take some time to work through. Even if you
are forgiving through gritted teeth and in obedience to the command
of Jesus, release will come to you as you are taking the hook out of
your flesh.

3. ACKNOWLEDGE YOUR FEELINGS

As we have seen when dealing with pain the healthy way to deal with your feelings is to:-

OWN THEM

   FEEL THEM

      EXPRESS THEM

         AND THEN DEAL WITH THE ISSUE.

Buried feelings will always cause problems, often years later.

There may be some really big feelings which will rattle around for some time even after you have decided to forgive. These are not a qualitative expression of how well you forgave! Feelings take time to dissipate.

DEALING WITH FEELINGS AND ISSUES CREATES UNDERSTANDING AND AUTHENTIC RELATIONSHIPS.

4. EVALUATE THE HURT AND ITS CONSEQUENCES

Sometimes we MINIMISE the consequences of another's actions upon us but we need to realistically assess the damage and the consequences to our lives that another's actions have caused. Acknowledging how bad it was for us may mean looking again at long held views. It is helpful to acknowledge that we are all damaged in some way. So to see the events that harmed you in the context of the life of the perpetrator, where they are now and the road they have travelled can be helpful, but this does not lessen or excuse what they may have done to you. Their difficult childhood may be a reason for their actions but it does not mean your wounding should be discounted.

Evaluation is taking a good look at the wound, the way a doctor would explore an old injury, understanding all the consequences before applying treatment. All we learnt in the 'How to deal with pain' chapter comes into play here too. This can take time.

Problems happen in relationships and we play our part too, so we need to be alive to our responsibility for the issue. However, big people do things to little people NOT the other way round; power resides with the big person, sometimes the child within us does not recognise that we were powerless.

5. BE WILLING TO CONFRONT THE OTHER PARTY
This is important to maintain healthy relations within the family, church , school, work and society at large. Each of us is like an iceberg as we move through life, only a small part is visible on the surface and our hidden depths are complex. What we are going through, our mood and our past experience are all in play when we interact with other people.

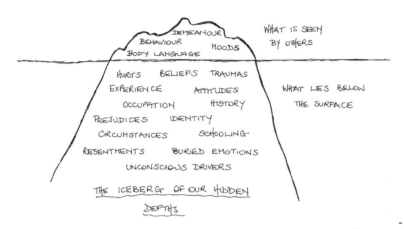

When we are faced with an uncomfortable situation we are programmed to go into 'fight or flight' mode. This can be both damaging and divisive but if we will take a risk and share our thinking and feelings; if we will be real with each other and are open about the pressures within us, we will grow deep and precious relationships. Conflict can be the catalyst that brings us closer together.

Sharing weaknesses strengthens bonds, loving each other where we are is powerful Kingdom living. Jesus modelled openness, self-awareness and transparency in relationships. Such vulnerability can transform churches for it allows us to come out from behind our masks and to start being real with one another.

However, what about confronting someone who has altered the course of our lives by their abuse of us? The principles may be the same but the repercussions will be much more complex as consequences roll down the years. It is a risky business to confront, not least because you cannot foretell the reactions of the other party when they are challenged. What if they do not accept 'anything happened'? It requires much preparation and wisdom to know whether confrontation is right. When we live in the Waterfall we can know that if we are to tackle someone from our past God will make it clear, otherwise leave it to Jesus.

HOW DO I DO THAT?
CONFRONTATION

If you are going to confront
- Prepare well. Be sure you feel it is right to confront.
- Never do it when you are angry or your feelings are raw.
- Own and deal with your energetic emotions, work through them so you understand why you feel and think as you do.
- Set a time and place to meet that is convenient and neutral.
- Relay in a non-accusatory way to the other person what you felt when the incident happened and its consequences for you.
- Invite the other person to share what was going on for them.
- Let compassion and love in. What would Jesus say and do here?
- Allow the other person to catch up, you have prepared for this. They may need some time to reframe their position as you share yours.
- Ask for forgiveness for your part.
- Forgive, it is the oil that lubricates relationships and binds us together. Agree to work on difficult issues.

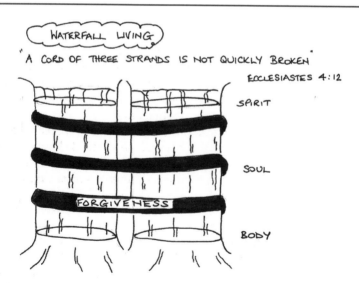

6. BE WILLING TO BE RECONCILED

Reconciliation is restoring the relationship, to fully accept again the other person. It leads to powerful testimony when people are willing to understand their differences, forgive and let go of their hurt, accept each other and move forward together. There have been extraordinary examples of this in The Peace Process in Northern Ireland and the Reconciliation Commission in South Africa after apartheid.

When we experience trouble, misunderstandings or mistakes in our relationships and go through the forgiveness process to this stage, we find those relationships become stronger as though forged in fire. We know each other more, know we can deal with problems, and trust and freedom are found together in a strong bond between us.

Again this stage requires wisdom and is not always possible. It takes two to restore a relationship and the other party may not be willing to do so. You are only responsible for your own actions and some else's inability to travel this road does not limit the freedom that is yours having forgiven them.

Our God is the God of families, they are precious to Him. The family is a divine structure and where He places us is no coincidence. My experience has been that when I work with an individual and they make the decision to walk in the Waterfall they begin to see change in their wider family, often leading to healing and reconciliation. This is the heart of God to see reconciliation in fractured families. The Gospel of Jesus Christ is the Gospel of peace and reconciliation through forgiveness.

7. BE FREE

To be free we must avail ourselves of the gift that Jesus gave us, seeking forgiveness and reaching out to others in forgiveness. It is not always easy and demands effort and often people worry whether they have really forgiven because memories and difficult feelings still pop up. If you have taken the decision to forgive, the deal is done and will not be revoked but we still may need to deal with the residual effects within us.

However, what if the person keeps sinning against us or we learn more of the effect it has had on us?

Well Jesus forgave even whilst He was being sinned against on the Cross so difficult though it may be He is our model. If we forgive some more it does not mean we did not forgive properly the first time but that we are now dealing with the additional hurts.

We may need to forgive ourselves. This can be hard for it means coming out of the victim mode and standing on what God is saying. It is common to hear people say, "I cannot forgive myself". The subtext to that is, "I am too bad to be forgiven by the death of Jesus," or put another way, "Jesus' sacrifice was not big enough for me." There is a lot of false pride in that! It leaves Jesus pinned to the Cross. There is NOTHING that cannot be covered by the blood of Jesus. We are called to live in the freedom that the Cross gives to please our heavenly Father. He cared so much 'that He sent the best thing He had to save us' as we sing in that chorus *'I'm special because God has loved me'* by Graham Kendrick. **It cost God for us to be free.**

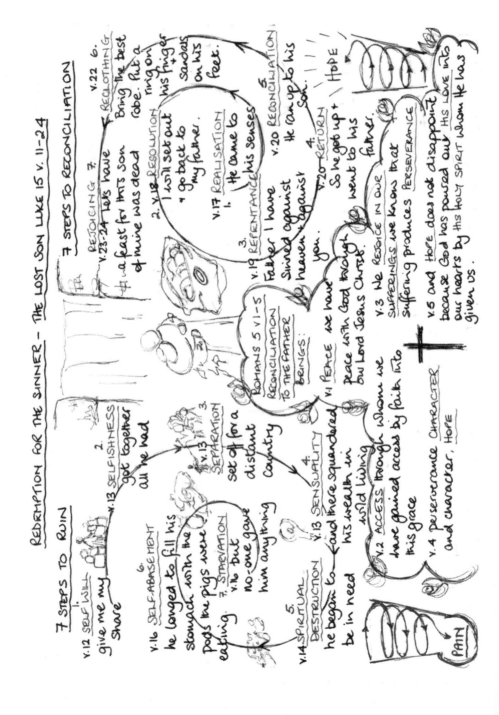

REDEMPTION FOR THE SINNER – THE LOST SON LUKE 15 V. 11-24

7 STEPS TO RUIN

1.
v.12 SELF WILL
give me my
share

2.
v.13 SELFISHNESS
got together
all he had

3.
SEPARATION
v.13
set off for a
distant
country

4.
SENSUALITY
v.13
and there squandered
his wealth in
wild living

5.
SPIRITUAL
DESTRUCTION v.14
he began to
be in need

6.
SELF-ABASEMENT
v.16
he longed to fill his
stomach with the
pods the pigs were
eating.

7. STARVATION
v.16 but
no-one gave
him anything

7 STEPS TO RECONCILIATION

1.
v.17 REALISATION
He came to
his senses

2.
v.18 RESOLUTION
I will set out
+ go back to
my father.

3.
v.19 REPENTANCE
Father I have
sinned against
heaven + against
you.

4.
v.20 RETURN
So he got up +
went to his
father.

5.
v.20 RECONCILIATION
He ran up to his
son.

6.
v.22 RE-CLOTHING
Bring the best
robe. Put a
ring on
his finger
+ sandals
on his
feet.

7.
REJOICING
v.23-24 Let's have
+ a feast for this son
of mine was dead

ROMANS 5 v1-5
RECONCILIATION
TO THE FATHER
BRINGS:

v.1 PEACE we have
peace with God through
our Lord Jesus Christ.

v.2 ACCESS through whom we
have gained access by faith into
this grace

v.3 He REJOICE IN OUR
SUFFERINGS we know that
suffering produces PERSEVERANCE

v.4 perseverance CHARACTER
and character, HOPE

v.4 perseverance CHARACTER
and character, HOPE

v.5 and HOPE does not disappoint
because God has poured out HIS LOVE INTO
our hearts by HIS HOLY SPIRIT whom He has
given us.

HOPE

PAIN

Notes

CONCLUSION

THE PRESENT AND THE FUTURE

We have been exploring throughout this book how to bring alive the teachings and life of Jesus, to give spiritual muscle to our own walk of discipleship on the Waterfall Journey.

As we travel the Waterfall Journey as disciples we are following the model of Jesus walking this earth and He gifted us with another clue to the essence of abiding in the presence of the Father when He said:

Peace I leave with you; my peace I give you. I do not give to you as the world gives. Do not let your hearts be troubled and do not be afraid. John 14:27

I owe my friend Phyll a debt for sharing her wisdom with me about God's peace. She said that when you begin to walk with the Lord you travel from hill top to valley bottom and your peace can ricochet up and down with the landscape but when you step into the Waterfall you are saying, "I trust you." Then life becomes a constant experience of internal peace as Jesus portrayed it, which flowed out of His rock-sure relationship with His Father and His knowing who He was and what He was about. HIS ABSOLUTE TRUST GAVE HIM ABSOLUTE PEACE.

THINK BIG
When Jesus was here on earth, God took ordinary men and women and because by choice they committed themselves completely to His will and purpose they became extra-ordinary. The church, the body of Christ expanded exponentially through ordinary people who believed God meant what He said. In our walk we have to struggle through the pull of the fallen world's values, ideas and enticements where control of our life seems the only way to survive.

BUT if we make the decision, exactly the same decision that the disciples made, and live abiding in God's presence as Jesus did in the Waterfall, God's astronomic scale of happenings comes into being. Twelve disciples changed the known world as they walked in the Waterfall. There after an apprenticeship learning to hear and obey and becoming trusted and faithful in Kingdom ways they found power, cause and effect flowing on God's scale. It means we too should think BIG.

If you are reading this, God is calling you to move on a scale that you probably will not comprehend until it happens but you need to lift your head and blast away anything that confines your thinking.

....

 *I met Pastor Sam on my first trip to Uganda in 2001 – he was blown away by the Waterfall and wanted his people to know about it. So the next year we added Masaka to our itinerary.*

The church was in a cow shed, a long low building which at one end housed Sam and his extended family and at the other end was used for services. Meetings were held under the mango tree at the far end of the building which was set in a dusty bowl of land. Maribou storks picked over a pile of rubbish on the town side and cattle wandered through.

We, Heather and I, had arrived on the Saturday after a long and electrifying drive from Kampala where we had had a busy week teaching. We were staying in a small hotel and Pastor Sam picked us up and took us to the church. It was early and I will not forget my first sight of the cow shed in the early morning light, nor of the walls which were painted with bright and wonderful murals. There were some hard wooden benches and one or two white plastic chairs and plenty of hard baked mud floor! There were three services, two in English and one in the local language and we shared the Waterfall at each one to great excitement, followed by a time of ministry. There were probably a hundred and fifty people there in total that morning.

One side of the shed was open to the expanse of land and when tired and hungry we made our way out later, I nearly fell over a pile of bricks. Sam explained this was the model of the three thousand seater church he was going to build on this land. It had two towers that would house the radio station, pastors' retreat centre, the counselling service and family and children's work. The auditorium would have a downstairs and an upper balcony. He had the plans but no money but he was just waiting for God to say, "Go!" It was a breathtaking vision to glorify God in a township where a huge mosque had been built that was extravagantly intimidating and intrusive.

For the next six years I went to Masaka each July. The first year there were some foundations and scaffolding and as I taught, the end of the cow shed was being demolished. Sam said he had heard from God one day saying that it was time to start building so he had just waited by the phone. A call came from a builder who needed some work starting the next Monday. Sam said yes he had a project and looking at the plans the builder drew up a list of the things he would need to start. Still with no money Sam waited. One phone call came and then another until by Saturday everything on the list was ready for the work to begin the following week.

Each year the auditorium grew. The pattern remained the same. Sam would hear God saying go ahead for the next stage and he would sit by the phone and wait. Sam always waited until God provided the materials and then the building would start. I have taught under dripping sheets of blue plastic whilst behind on the platform the vivid and vibrant murals were being painted on the backdrop and in front was a building site. Year on year it slowly rose from the dust. For various personal reasons I have not been back to Uganda since 2009 but I have this year seen the photos as the balcony is being completed.

Sam has a huge and influential ministry that he would tell you was radically changed by understanding the Waterfall. To speak with him is inspiring as he sees no limits in working shoulder to shoulder with the Living God, so that God does mighty things through him. The BIG has come a step at a time but Sam has never failed to take each pace forward however unlikely it has looked.

THE ELEMENTS OF THE WATERFALL JOURNEY

It's understanding God's story and our part in it.

It's where you stand, abiding in the Father's presence.

It's being the channel of the living God every moment of the day.

It's where all things work for good.

It's drawing your identity from Him.

It's seeking the fullness of Jesus and all that the Cross means.

It's understanding the roles of the Trinity.

It's choosing God's will and purpose for your life and trusting Him for every aspect of it.

It's listening, knowing His voice and obeying.

It's recognising sin and knowing the cleansing of forgiveness.

It's maturing, journeying and being willing to go through the narrow gate.

It is being the friend of Jesus, not a servant, but on the team.

It's allowing Jesus to renew the mind and to be open to inner healing.

It is being equipped for your full ministry.

However, some years into my journey, God woke me in the early hours of one morning and in half an hour gave me the vision of Beyond the Waterfall, which was electrifying and exciting. It showed me how limited my thoughts had been. I felt an urgency to share what was flowing so I tried to rush things and experimented with sharing The Waterfall Journey and Beyond the Waterfall together but it was not successful. Repenting, I waited for God and He showed me that trust and character need to be forged in the reality of living in His presence so that we are ready for the higher calling beyond.

What I share is God's heart for His people and He is calling you to experience life this way, with Him as a foundation for the next stage which is Beyond the Waterfall.

At the moment in churches there are many sincere people who are not disciples; the majority are unaware of how damaged they are. *Rick Joyner's "The Call"* graphically illustrates how blind we can be to the situation. Many, in being saved, do not have the teaching or the soul friend to walk beside them as they move through to full discipleship. Following the Waterfall Journey will take people along the path to maturity. I believe it will be people, each walking in the Waterfall and joining up together, that will bring the church to readiness for battle and to purity to be the Bride of Christ. The Waterfall Journey is based on that belief.

BEYOND THE WATERFALL

It's about coming up higher and dwelling in the throne room.

It's practising the presence of God.

It's living in God's perspective day by day.

It's maturity on the journey, building character and holiness in the sum of our choices.

It's army structures with an urgency to train the army of the Lord.

It's holding ground, understanding borders, taking possession.

It's understanding the structures of heaven – and spiritual warfare.

It's acting in authority with power.

It's different forms of prayer, reaping and sowing, binding and loosing.

It's creating inheritance, passing on experience.

It is being heaven's ambassadors – ruling and reigning.

It is God out of the box and us free of constraints.

It's being naturally supernatural with flourishing gifts.

It's dancing and flying.

It is wearing the mantle of Jesus.

My prayer is that you meet God within these pages to ever deeper levels that you might become all that He designed you to be and accomplish all that He planned for you to do for His honour and glory.

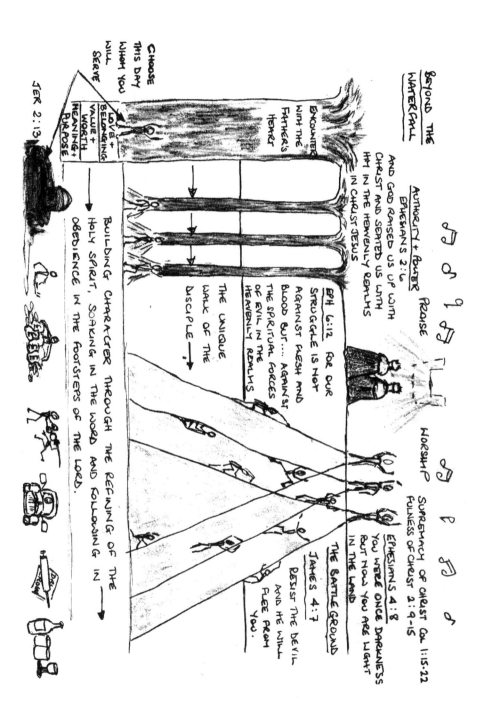

BEYOND THE WATERFALL

CHOOSE THIS DAY WHOM YOU WILL SERVE

JER 2:13

ENCOUNTER WITH THE FATHER'S HEART

LOVE + BELONGING
WORTH + VALUE
MEANING + PURPOSE

AUTHORITY + POWER   PRAISE
EPHESIANS 2:6
AND GOD RAISED US UP WITH CHRIST AND SEATED US UP WITH HIM IN THE HEAVENLY REALMS IN CHRIST JESUS

EPH 6:12 FOR OUR STRUGGLE IS NOT AGAINST FLESH AND BLOOD BUT... AGAINST THE SPIRITUAL FORCES OF EVIL IN THE HEAVENLY REALMS

THE UNIQUE WALK OF THE DISCIPLE →

BUILDING CHARACTER THROUGH THE REFINING OF THE HOLY SPIRIT, SOAKING IN THE WORD AND FOLLOWING IN OBEDIENCE IN THE FOOTSTEPS OF THE LORD.

WORSHIP

SUPREMACY OF CHRIST COL 1:15-22
FULLNESS OF CHRIST 2:9-15

EPHESIANS 4:8
YOU WERE ONCE DARKNESS BUT NOW YOU ARE LIGHT IN THE LORD

THE BATTLE GROUND

JAMES 4:7
RESIST THE DEVIL AND HE WILL FLEE FROM YOU.

215

BIBLIOGRAPHY

BOOKS MENTIONED OR SIGNIFICANT ON MY JOURNEY

Finding God — Larry Crabb
Christ Empowered Living — Selwyn Hughes
How to hear God's Voice — Mark Virkler
The Final Quest — Rick Joyner
The Call — Rick Joyner
When Heaven invades Earth — Bill Johnston
The Supernatural Power of the Transformed Mind — Bill Johnston
God's Story — Philip Greenslade
God Calling by the Two — Anon
Christ Stress and Glory — Wanda Nash
The Message — Eugene Peters
Chasing the Dragon — Jackie Pullinger

APPENDIX

The Father's Love Letter

My Child...
You may not know me, but I know everything about you... *Psalm 139:1*
I know when you sit down and when you rise up... *Psalm 139:2*
I am familiar with all your ways... *Psalm 139:3*
Even the very hairs on your head are numbered... *Matthew 10:29-31*
For you were made in my image... *Genesis 1:27*
In me you live and move and have your being... *Acts 17:28*
For you are my offspring... *Acts 17:28*
I knew you even before you were conceived... *Jeremiah 1:4-5*
I chose you when I planned creation... *Ephesians 1:11-12*
You were not a mistake... *Psalm 139:15-16*
For all your days are written in my book... *Psalm 139:15-16*
I determined the exact time of your birth and where you would live... *Acts 17:26*
You are fearfully and wonderfully made... *Psalm 139:14*
I knit you together in your mother's womb... *Psalm 139:13*
And brought you forth on the day you were born... *Psalm 71:6*
I have been misrepresented by those who don't know me... *John 8:41-44*
I am not distant and angry, but am the complete expression of love... *1 John 4:16*
And it is my desire to lavish my love on you...1 John 3:1
Simply because you are my child and I am your Father... *1 John 3:1*
I offer you more than your earthly father ever could... *Matthew 7:11*
For I am the perfect Father... *Matthew 5:48*
Every good gift that you receive comes from my hand... *James 1:17*
For I am your provider and I meet all your needs... *Matthew 6:31-33*
My plan for your future has always been filled with hope... *Jeremiah 29:11*
Because I love you with an everlasting love... *Jeremiah 31:3*
My thoughts toward you are countless as the sand on the seashore... *Psalm 139:17-18*
And I rejoice over you with singing... *Zephaniah 3:17*
I will never stop doing good to you... *Jeremiah 32:40*
For you are my treasured possession... *Exodus 19:5*
I desire to establish you with all my heart and all my soul... *Jeremiah 32:41*
And I want to show you great and marvellous things... *Jeremiah 33:3*
If you seek me with all your heart, you will find me... *Deuteronomy 4:29*
Delight in me and I will give you the desires of your heart... *Psalm 37:4*
For it is I who gave you those desires... *Philippians 2:13*
I am able to do more for you than you could possibly imagine... *Ephesians 3:20*
For I am your greatest encourager... *2 Thessalonians 2:16-17*
I am also the Father who comforts you in all your troubles... *2 Corinthians 1:3-4*

When you are broken-hearted, I am close to you... *Psalm 34:18*
As a shepherd carries a lamb, I have carried you close to my heart... *Isaiah 40:11*
One day I will wipe away every tear from your eyes... *Revelation 21:3-4*
And I'll take away all the pain you have suffered on this earth... *Revelation 21:4*
I am your Father and I love you even as I love my son, Jesus... *John 17:23*
For in Jesus my love for you is revealed... *John 17:26*
He is the exact representation of my being... *Hebrews 1:3*
And He came to demonstrate that I am for you, not against you... *Romans 8:31*
And to tell you that I am not counting your sins... *2 Corinthians 5:18-19*
Jesus died so that you and I could be reconciled... *2 Corinthians 5:18-19*
His death was the ultimate expression of my love for you... *1 John 4:10*
I gave up everything I loved that I might gain your love... *Romans 8:32*
If you receive the gift of my son Jesus, you receive me... *1 John 2:23*
And nothing will ever separate you from my love again... *Romans 8:38-39*
Come home and I'll throw the biggest party heaven has ever seen... *Luke 15:7*
I have always been Father and will always be Father... *Ephesians 3:14-15*
My question is...Will you be my child?... *John 1:12-13*
I am waiting for you... *Luke 15:11-32*

Love, Your Dad
Almighty God

Notes

Notes

Diagrams